# Bernd Degen

The planet Earth is the only known heavenly body in our solar system that contains liquid water. About 75% of the Earth's surface is covered by water. At one time all of the Earth was probably covered by water. This means that every living thing on the Earth originated in the waters of the Earth...including us. Remember, before we are born, we are actually swimming in our mother's placenta, just like fish.

In the Earth's waters are to be found between 20,000 and 30,000 species of fishes. Certainly, for

The Rio Negro, a typical "black water" tributary of the Amazon system. Photo by the author.

aquarists, some of the most interesting of these fishes are contained in the genus *Symphysodon*, the discus fishes. What has made these fish so popular? Certainly the fact that they were so difficult to breed had a lot to do with their expense and not until the later 1960's were there any successful commercial breeders of discus. Now almost anyone can breed discus, especially after studying this book, and they can make a profit by selling their home-bred fish to their local petshop.

Another factor in making discus so popular is that they are peaceful, probably the most

**The author at home on the Rio Negro, using reverse osmosis apparatus to prepare a water sample for chemical testing back in Germany.**

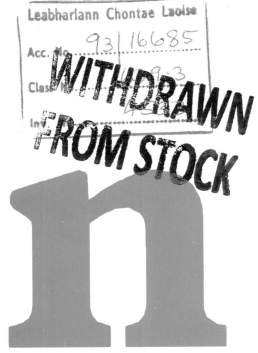

peaceful fish for their size that is common in the aquarium.

The final major factor that makes discus fish so interesting is that they easily hybridize with other fishes in the same genus and produce magnificent color variations, body shape variations and finnage variations.

Now discus are found in many colors, shapes and finnages thanks to the great discus breeders in Germany (Dr. Eduard Schmidt-Focke and Bernd Degen), the American Jack Wattley, and a score of breeders in Hong Kong, Singapore, Thailand and Taiwan.

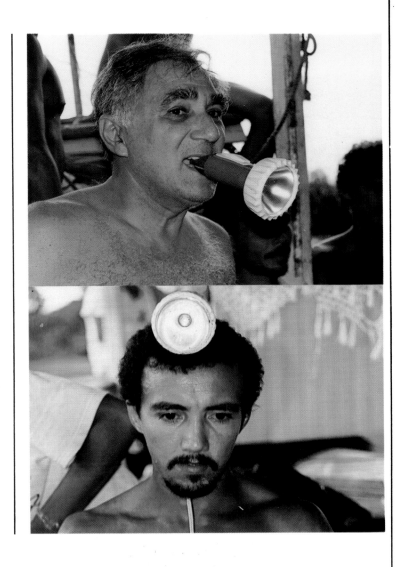

**Discus fishermen use a variety of flashlights and lanterns to collect discus at night. Dr. Axelrod (top) models one of the most acceptable ways of holding a lantern. Photos by Dr. H. R. Axelrod.**

**Dr. Herbert R. Axelrod, standing; Jack Wattley, left with the author, right.**

I know the author, Bernd Degen, very well. Every word in this book is written from the bottom of his heart. He breeds discus. He loves discus. He lives discus. I can securely highly recommend this book for anyone interested in discus.

*Dr. Herbert R. Axelrod*

Book

# Foreword

This, my second discus book, is conceived with much love. It is my hope that it will impart the experience of my years of keeping discus and provide practical hints for discus fanciers.

For the last 20 years I have been enthusiastically involved with discus and have imported wild-caught discus, traveling to their home countries to get the most beautiful specimens for my special breeding aims. Of course, even today I not only have good times but also grave hours with some failures. But once infected with discus fever, there is no escape.

The author, Bernd Degen. Photo by Dr. H. R. Axelrod.

© Copyright 1990 by T.F.H. Publications, Inc.

Distributed in the UNITED STATES by T.F.H. Publications, Inc., One T.F.H. Plaza, Neptune City, NJ 07753; in CANADA to the Pet Trade by H & L Pet Supplies Inc., 27 Kingston Crescent, Kitchener, Ontario N2B 2T6; Rolf C. Hagen Ltd., 3225 Sartelon Street, Montreal 382 Quebec; in CANADA to the Book Trade by Macmillan of Canada (A Division of Canada Publishing Corporation), 164 Commander Boulevard, Agincourt, Ontario M1S 3C7; in ENGLAND by T.F.H. Publications Limited, Cliveden House/Priors Way/Bray, Maidenhead, Berkshire SL6 2HP, England; in AUSTRALIA AND THE SOUTH PACIFIC by T.F.H. (Australia) Pty. Ltd., Box 149, Brookvale 2100 N.S.W., Australia; in NEW ZEALAND by Ross Haines & Son, Ltd., 82 D Elizabeth Knox Place, Panmure, Auckland, New Zealand; in the PHILIPPINES by Bio-Research, 5 Lippay Street, San Lorenzo Village, Makati Rizal; in SOUTH AFRICA by Multipet Pty. Ltd., Box 235 New Germany, South Africa 3620. Published by T.F.H. Publications, Inc. Manufactured in the United States of America by T.F.H. Publications, Inc.

**The author displaying part of his modern and spacious fishroom.**

Today, my primary aim is the breeding of the best of these fishes. In my home I have two rooms with a total of 20 aquaria in which to perform studies on discus, and the results can be passed on to all my discus friends. The value of discus breeding is, for me, to maintain a high quality standard in breeding and to promote the best concepts of crossbreeding.

I hope that this book will give you much pleasure and that its hints will help make you successful. If so, it certainly will have achieved its real aim.

Bernd Degen

**Buckram-reinforced Library Binding**

•

**Patent Number 4,106,148**

•

**Additional Patents Pending**

**T.F.H. PUBLICATIONS, INC.**
**1 T.F.H. Plaza • Third and Union Aves. • Neptune City, NJ 07753**

# CONTENTS

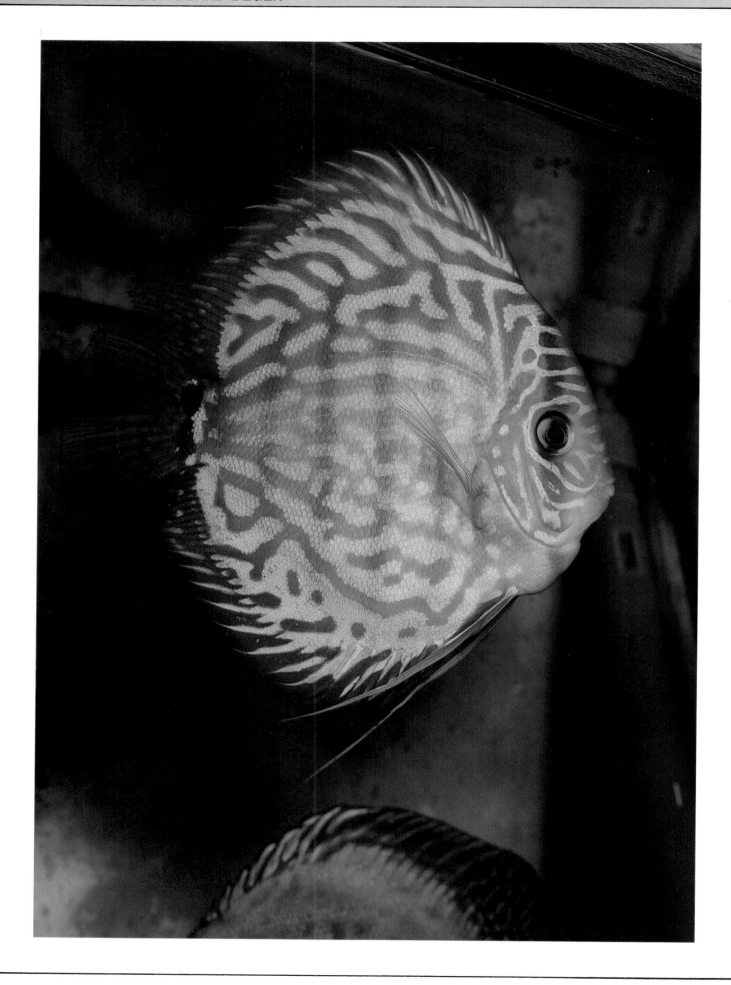

# Origin of discus

The original home of the discus species (two currently recognized as valid, *Symphysodon aequifasciata* and *S. discus*, each with subspecies) is the Amazon River system, mainly in Brazil but also from Peru and Colombia. The Amazon River may bring to mind the cliché of a "green hell," but it is much more. The gigantic Amazon system with its millions of square kilometers of drainage and hundreds of

The author's chartered fishing boat on the Rio Negro. Compared to some fishing boats, this was a true luxury liner. Photo by the author.

tributary rivers is one of the largest and most stable biotopes on earth. The course of the river may be divided into three basic types. The loam-yellow or "white" upper Amazon, including the Rio Solimoes, Rio Purus, Rio Madeira, and Rio Jurua, rises in the Andes. The eastern or lower Amazon is the green-yellow or "clear water" river, including the Rio Xingu, Rio Tapajos, and Rio Araguaia. The central Amazon is a "black water" river, including mainly the Rio Negro flowing into the Amazon at Manaus.

The various types of water yield different kinds and colors of discus, but the entire Amazon system has the same low conductance, indicating a lack of minerals, which is an important fact to be considered in breeding, as hard waters would adversely influence or even stop breeding. The pH values of the "black water" area are about 4.0, while those of the "clear" and "white" sections are between 6.0 and 7.0. During the whole year the

Left: The wonderful form and personality of the discus has made it the king of aquarium fishes. Photo by the author of a beautiful turquoise specimen with interesting markings.

Behind the scenes at a discus-collecting operation on the Amazon. 1) The lanterns operate from car batteries attached through make-shift cables. 2) Small boats allow the collector to approach discus in very shallow water. 3) Often the entire family participates in the collecting business. 4) Preliminary sorting of the catch. 5) Plastic boxes and other equipment leave barely enough room for hammocks in the hold of the boat. Photos by Dr. H. R. Axelrod on the Rio Negro.

**Dr. Axelrod participating in a discus hunt on the Rio Negro. Fishing at night on the Amazon is no picnic—caimans, stingrays, and even the occasional jaguar are no joke.**

**The collected discus usually are kept in small netted enclosures along the river banks. This system allows most specimens to remain in good health until they are collected by the wholesaler. Photo by the author.**

temperature of the water is about 30°C (86°F), but there often are fluctuations due to heavy rainfall and flooding, which may have an effect on the discus's spawning behavior.

Normally the wild discus are sought at night by a collector using a flashlight or lantern, the light dazzling the discus so that they can be netted easily. They are held locally for a few days in plastic tanks and then transported to a dealer who may work out of Manaus or another major port, where they are held for up to several weeks in large concrete tanks with several thousand liters (about 4 liters per gallon) of

A gorgeous group of discus in a planted tank and carefully planned low light. Photo by the author.

water. Unfortunately, this long storage in concrete often leads to infections and the captives seldom eat well. Therefore, if you purchase a wild-caught discus, a period of quarantine will be necessary and it will have to be given exceptionally good care.

The temperature of the discus aquarium should not be below 27°C (81°F), and the breeding temperature should be about 30°C (86°F). Hard water must be softened. The normal conductance value is below 100 microSiemens (mS), but it can be a little higher. The pH value should be about 6.0 to be ideal, but on no account should the pH be over 7.0. Fluctuations in water chemistry may lead to damage of the color in young fish.

A varied diet is essential and should contain all the necessary proteins, carbohydrates, vitamins, and minerals. A healthy discus greedily eats all the usual foods if it has the proper aquarium conditions, and it even may be "trained" to eat out of its owner's hand. If you offer your discus the proper care and foods, you certainly will gain much pleasure from your fish.

# The culture system

## Basic filtering systems

Most discus fanciers do not keep just a single show aquarium but enough aquaria to enable them to also look forward to breeding their fantastic fish. Two basic systems of aquarium maintenance are used, each of which has its own advantages and disadvantages.

separately if it is necessary to change the water or medicate the tank. Your pet shop will have available numerous appropriate sizes and styles of filters (canisters, pads, biofilters, etc.) and pumps from which you can choose. Be sure to discuss your aims with your dealer first so you can plan for growth and added sophistication of your system as you become a more experienced keeper.

**Because discus tanks are best kept without a substrate, plants can be added in pots for easy maintenance. Photo by the author.**

In the most common system, several single aquaria 60 cm long by 50 cm deep by 50 cm high (24 x 20 x 20 inches) are put on appropriately sturdy stands or shelving. As they never should be totally filled, their capacity is about 130 L (33.8 gallons) of water, sufficient for two adult fish.

For a filtering system, good success can be had by using foam pads and a good air pump. Up to eight or ten foam pads can be handled by a strong air pump with a capacity of 1000 L (260 gallons). The filtering of four or five aquaria thus can be achieved by a strong pump able to handle two filters per aquarium. The advantage of such a method is that each of the aquaria can be treated

If the aquarium is too heavily planted, it becomes difficult to see the discus on demand. Photo by the author.

Large, properly planted tanks containing a few of the most beautiful discus make excellent displays. Photo by the author.

Another possibility is erecting a closed system of several aquaria sharing one filtering system. Your pet dealer offers or can obtain many types of plastic tubing with all the necessary rubber and plastic fittings, angles, T-joints, sleeves, and so on to set up a complete filtering system easily. Because you will be dealing with large amounts of water and will have to have aquaria drilled to accept tubing, do not attempt to start this system until you have carefully planned it and discussed it at length with your dealer or with another aquarist who has such a system. A small miscalculation can lead to serious problems and overflows—and dead fish.

In a basic closed system each aquarium is drilled to receive the proper size and number of inflow and outflow tubes plus emergency overflow tubes. Provision has to be made to prevent backflow to the filter if the power is lost, which would result in each tank attempting to drain itself into the next tank. Dealing with glass and plastic is not easy, and the essential emergency systems may be complicated, so I cannot emphasize too greatly advance planning and discussions with a knowledgeable dealer.

The water is pulled through the tubes into the central filter, which has to be large enough to handle all the aquaria. I use foam pad filters and floss as the basic media and also take the opportunity to treat the chemistry of the water with appropriate ion exchange resins. The last process is to pump the water back into the aquarium, normally done by using pumps of a high capacity but as energy-efficient as possible. A tube above the aquaria returns the filtered water to all the single aquaria. You thus may be sure that all the filtered water reflowing into the aquaria is chemically identical.

The advantage of the closed system is less work and nearly no servicing. The disadvantage is that all aquaria will be contaminated in case of sickness. Installing an ultraviolet lamp into the system will help as it will kill most bacteria. New styles of UV lamps on the market have waterproof electrical systems and can be installed easily into the circular course to secure almost pathogen-free filtered water. This system also is more expensive to initiate than the basic system and may be less flexible about adding and removing tanks.

Of course, any filtering system has the disadvantage that young fish can be drawn into the filter. Therefore, it is necessary to install a security system, as for example a cap of stainless wire mesh put over the intake, outflow, and overflow tubes.

One final hint—in order to avoid visual contact between breeding fish and the outside world, paper or opaque plastic should be placed between or around the aquaria. Disturbances such as seeing an "enemy" (=you) outside or threatening fish in an adjacent aquarium may cause some breeders to abort spawning or even eat already laid eggs.

**Healthy fry of a pearl red by brilliant turquoise mating feeding on the sides of the male. Cleanliness of water is essential for proper breeding of all discus. Photo by the author.**

# Water chemistry

## Water chemistry

Water is the living element of the discus, so the keeper should strive to control the hardness, pH, mineralization, and ammonia levels to maintain nearly natural conditions.

*sulfate hardness* based on the presence of soluble compounds such as calcium sulfate. Ion exchange resins operate by "trading" insoluble elements such as iron and magnesium for soluble elements such as sodium.

Another indication of hardness is conductance, which is the measure of the ability of an electrical current to travel through the water. Conductance is indicated in

### Hardness

Normally, most discus fanciers have only tap water at their disposal, and it usually is sufficient providing it is not too hard. Hardness may be measured in several ways, but we will use German values, where 1°dH (degree of German hardness) is equivalent to the presence of 1 gram of soluble calcium oxide or equivalent in 100 L (26 gallons) of water. Based on this scale, hardness can be stated in more general terms:

0—4° dH = very soft
4—8° dH = soft
8—12° dH = medium soft
12—18° dH = medium hard
18—30° dH = hard
over 30° dH = very hard.

There actually are two types of hardness, *carbonate hardness* measuring hardness due to carbonates producing insoluble deposits (scale), and

The recent perfection of ion exchange resins has made the life of the discus breeder much simpler. Now he can produce water of any softness and chemistry he needs. Photo by the author.

**The black waters of the Rio Negro produce a splendid panorama but can be very difficult to duplicate in the aquarium. Photo by the author.**

units known as microSiemens or mS; the greater the mS, the more mineralized the water and (usually) the greater its hardness. Very soft water has difficulty carrying a current.

The rivers of the Amazon system are very soft, with a conductance value of lower than 100 mS and with virtually no calcium sulfate. "Black water" normally is very dark, with a pH lower than 5.0 and with many dissolved organic elements. These elements include many humic acids from plant decomposition that are the basis for the very low pH.

Water hardness is easily measured by various types of testing kits available from your pet dealer. Some measure German hardness directly, others parts per million (ppm) of dissolved substances, while still others determine concentrations of specific dissolved elements. All can be converted to the dH scale. A hardness test kit is an essential item for any aquarist.

It is not quite true to say that we need soft water for our discus, as domestically bred discus have adapted to harder waters than their wild cousins and can be kept even in tap water with a hardness of about 15° dH. This degree of hardness and a temperature of about 28 to 30°C (82-86°F) will lead to smaller problems than the use of very soft water that generally is very unstable and constantly changing in its pH.

Nevertheless, the *breeding water* has to be very soft. If sufficiently soft water is not available, it is necessary to "desalt" it down to a value below 1° dH. The carbonate hardness may be desalted by an appropriate cation exchange resin. Consult your pet dealer for the resins appropriate to your local water. Often two different resins must be used in combination, one to remove undesirable elements and the other to replace the temporary chemistry with a more desirable element. Ion exchange chemistry is complex—seek professional help. Do not attempt to completely desalt the water because "pure" water is extremely acidic and lacks the various chemicals necessary to sustain aquatic life. It will be necessary to measure and, if necessary, correct the pH of desalted water to the appropriate level. Again, consult your dealer for the necessary test kits and chemicals. Desalted water often is mixed with untreated aquarium water to help stabilize the pH and assure that essential minerals are present. Any changes in the water chemistry can produce a stress reaction in the discus and should be made slowly and with continual testing of the parameters being changed.

An old way to reduce the hardness of the water is peat filtering, which works somewhat like ion exchange resins. It is essential that you use the right peat with no fertilizer added. To be sure, soak one spoonful of peat overnight in 0.25 L (0.5 pint) of water and test it for ammonium and nitrates. In use, 0.5 L (1 pint) of peat in 100 L (26 gallons) of water should be changed after one or two weeks.

**Nitrates and pH**

Unfortunately, most of our discus are kept in bad water. They do not do well and remain in a corner of the aquarium. The water has to be free of high nitrates, below 30 ppm. With many tap water sources now containing 50 ppm and more, this means that treatment is essential. Because plants usually need high nitrate levels and also produce nitrates through decomposition, tanks containing plants may need constant water changes.

Special resins can be used to control nitrate level (see your dealer for details). As this method removes nitrites, nitrates, and some carbonate hardness, it can be used to produce water that is excellent for raising discus.

Heavy feeding naturally will lead to an increase of nitrates and eventually to an increase of ammonium compounds. As long as the pH is below 7.0, the ammonium is not especially dangerous and doesn't change to the poisonous ammonia, a change that does not happen until the pH exceeds 6.8. This would mean that the pH of new water always has to be controlled in the case of larger water changes. It is very simple to remove ammonium or ammonia by partial changes of water, which should have a pH below 6.8.

The pH of the water is a mathematical ratio based on the relative number of ions of

The silent killer—pH shock. Photo by the author.

bases (hydroxides) and acids (hydroxyls). A neutral value is 7.0, with values from 0 to 6.9 being acidic and values of 7.1 to 14 being basic. The suggested values for keeping discus are between 5.5 and 7.0, and between 5.5 and 6.5 for breeding purposes. Small changes in pH values reflect large changes in the number of ions. This is because in the pH scale each full number of the scale represents a ten-fold increase in the number of ions. For example, water with a pH of 5.0 contains (relatively) ten times as many hydroxyl (acid) ions as water with a pH of 6.0. Large fluctuations of the pH should be avoided. In planted aquaria you will have an acidic pH due to carbonic acid formed from plant respiration.

The pH may be reduced by phosphoric acid, but this process obviously has to be done using the proper equipment and only in carefully measured steps. 10 ml (0.3 fluid ounces) of a 10 percent solution of this acid should be enough when slowly dripped into the water and measured after each addition. In pet shops a small apparatus to diminish the pH may be available. An increase of the pH value can be made by adding sodium hydroxide. However, both of these non-biological methods are not ideal and it would be better to diminish the pH by instantly decreasing the carbonate hardness. As this decrease should not be below 3° dH, it is of no great use for breeding purposes, where you should instead look to peat filtering to decrease the pH.

Still another method of decreasing pH is the use of carbonic acid, but in the case of breeding aquaria the only effective method is peat filtering with humic acids to get a natural "black water." A too low pH can be controlled by carbonic acid along with very strong filtering. By increasing the carbonate hardness an increase of pH is achieved that is no problem in normal aquaria but is a problem in breeding aquaria due to problems of lime.

**Temperature**

One requirement of healthy discus is a constant water temperature of 27–28°C (81–82°F). Even a temperature of just 25–26°C (77–79°F), usually considered suitable for plants, will reduce feeding activity and cause darkening of the fish's colors. In their natural habitats discus often are found in temperatures as high as 32°C (90°F).

**Ultraviolet lamps**

For a long time I have been searching for a good method of disinfecting the water that will be gentle, efficient, involve no chemicals or antibiotics, and have no dangerous secondary effects. The UV lamp seems to fulfill these criteria.

Light is a combination of rays of different wavelengths. The human eye can detect wavelengths between 400 and 700 nm (nanometers, 1/1,000,000 mm). The wavelength of infrared rays (heat) and radio is above 800 nm, much longer than either the visible spectrum or the very short UV and X-rays.

The physiological effects of ultraviolet light depend on the wavelength. Full-spectrum UV is composed of three wavelength ranges:

UV–A, 315 to 400 nm;
UV–B, 280 to 315 nm; and
UV–C, 200 to 280 nm.

The UV–C rays are the most important rays for sterilization. The UV equipment on the market normally produces rays of 254 nm.

The special effects of UV–C can be seen in molecular biology. Nucleic acids (comprising DNA, parts of chromosomes, genes, etc.) are present in the water in bacteria, spores, fungi, yeast, and similar cells. These cells differentially absorb rays in the range of 254 nm. The energy of this wavelength causes chemical changes in the nucleic acids similar to those produced by cooking (denaturation of proteins). The protein molecules are destroyed, causing immediate death of the cells.

The usual UV sterilizer consists of a UV lamp in a UV-transparent glass cylinder. The space between the cylinder and the lamp is filled with water passing through from the filter. The UV sterilizer should be installed into the return flow from the filter, preferably in a special by-pass so that part of the water is treated before flowing into the aquarium. In order to obtain high efficiency, it is necessary to use very clean water. Humic acids, detritus, and natural dyes will impair the efficiency of the UV rays.

The flow speed and depth of the layer of water passing around the lamp are important parameters for efficient use. The flow speed is diminished by the by-pass, and the thickness of the water film is based on the diameter of the cylinder. Normally, an apparatus operating at 8 to 10 watts is not sufficient. The lamp should operate at at least 20 watts. The UV lamp should be changed after continuous use for seven to eight months as its efficiency will by then be only 10%.

Complete sterilization of the water is not possible and also is not recommended as the water should remain biologically active and a decrease in number of harmful cells is completely sufficient. Remember that bacteria are essential to decomposition processes and thus to life in the water.

UV sterilizers are a great help in quarantine aquaria, in which new fish should be held for a while. Due to transport stress and injuries, new fish normally are somewhat weak, and water with fewer bacteria may help them recover faster.

There is controversy as to whether UV sterilizers should be on continually. Many aquarists are afraid of side-effects and operate their sterilizers for only a few hours a day. Certainly continual operation of a UV lamp cannot be allowed in a small system or in individual aquaria containing few fish. In such circumstances continual use may cause the fish to lose their powers of resistance to bacterial infections. When a change of water is made they will be more subject to invasion by water-borne bacteria. Therefore in small systems or single aquaria only limited use of a UV sterilizer is recommended. The continual use of UV sterilizers is recommended only for large systems with central filtering in order to avoid infections spreading from one aquarium to another.

Because UV rays cause changes in molecular chemistry, they cannot be left on if medicines are added to the water. This is because they could cause changes in chemical structure of medicines based on organic molecules and effectively neutralize the medication. Also, if the nitrate level of the water is high, UV lights must be turned off. They cause nitrates to change into poisonous nitrites.

# Feeding strategies

## Basic requirements

The behavior of discus clearly depends on their feeding, but only the basics of their natural requirements are known today. As in all other living things, food is the basis of their growth and development (which also are influenced by genetic qualities), color, sex, and size. If discus are, for example, fed

over a long time only on meat, there would be internal damage, vitamin deficiencies, and probably hormonal imbalances. Discus must be fed a very varied diet. In Brazil, for instance, they often feed on small shrimp and other crustaceans that have fed on algae and other plants, proving that discus need a food rich in plant proteins and other constituents, even if they get them indirectly. The carotene (orange pigment) in the shrimp influences the color of the wild discus, a condition difficult to achieve by substitute foods.

Some constituents of the food are used for energy (such as movement) and other parts provide the chemicals necessary for growth and basic metabolism. Because the discus is "cold-blooded," deriving energy from its environment rather than creating it internally, little metabolic energy is necessary to maintain its temperature as it floats in the warm water. Discus may remain alive and minimally active for long periods without feeding. A surplus of food may lead to accumulations of fats and starches in the liver.

Of course, the food must contain the essential vitamins and minerals that are so necessary for all metabolic chemistry. Essential for growth are amino acids contained in the proteins of

**Healthy discus constantly are on the prowl for food, checking each bit of bottom debris for edibility. Photo by the author.**

**Unlike beef heart, the author's special food based on turkey heart is not only loved by the fish but has no bad side-effects. Photo by the author.**

fishes, crustaceans, and other animal foods. Some fats (contained in the natural food) are necessary for chemical reactions, but additional amounts should not be given. Carbohydrates (sugars, starches, and cellulose) that cannot be quickly digested are stored for later use. Cellulose is important for proper bowel movements.

A balanced diet must provide enough vitamin, carbohydrates, fats, animal proteins, and minerals such as calcium, magnesium, chlorine, sodium, phosphorus, and sulphur. The trace elements iron, manganese, copper, fluorine, iodine, zinc, cobalt, and selenium can be taken from the food but also can be absorbed through the skin and gills. The water of the aquarium should always contain these trace elements, one reason it is wrong to totally demineralize the water.

Feeding and bowel function are influenced by the oxygen absorbed from the water, especially in the case of high water temperatures and stress. Discus should not be fed for 12 to 24 hours before they are shipped, and even 48 hours is not too long if they are large specimens.

Discus are omnivorous (feeding on both plant and animal matter), so it is very easy to adapt them to almost any food available if it is appropriate. After four weeks they should be used to almost any food, but be patient if you must change the food for any reason. Normally discus prefer to feed from the bottom. It is very important that the size of the food should be small, as discus bolt their food without chewing.

As we often cannot offer living foods, frozen foods are quite acceptable. As is the case with any new food, it is important that the discus get

to know the new food and learn to wait for it at feeding time.

The lighting system is very important. The light should be turned on at least half an hour before feeding and should remain on for at least one hour after feeding.

Young fish fed on brine shrimp nauplii should be monitored closely and given supplements of yeast, vitamins and minerals, or algae to ensure they get a complete diet.

**Specific foods**

A standard food for discus that are half-grown or fully grown is the larvae of various flies, especially mosquito larvae, bloodworms, and glassworms. While the various brands of frozen larvae available in pet shops generally are quite satisfactory, living larvae are better but often impossible to get. Most frozen larvae offered are bloodworms, which in my opinion really are not as good for the fish as mosquito larvae and glassworms. One advantage of feeding frozen foods is purity—you do not have to worry about contamination with parasites, micropredators, or many types of bacteria. The possibility of chemical contamination with pesticides or heavy metals remains, but the same problem is found with living food.

One disadvantage of frozen foods is that the larvae tend to remain on the water surface and rarely sink. Of course, discus prefer to take their food from the bottom.

Besides the feeding of larval flies, many discus breeders like to feed beef heart, which has the disadvantage of having large fibers that may lead to constipation. I prefer to make my own frozen food based on turkey heart enriched with vitamins and

**A wide variety of frozen foods is available at your pet shop. Most are quite good, although each type may have its drawbacks. Photo by the author.**

minerals. It does not foul the water and is composed of very fine fibers.

Advantages of frozen foods include simple handling and ready availability, but don't forget that leftovers rapidly foul the water. Pieces of beef heart in the water will lead to nearly immediate putrefaction and therefore should be removed quickly.

Beef heart normally has the fat removed and then is cut into pieces and minced in a blender, but it also is possible to freeze whole pieces and mince them with a grinding mill on demand. For this I recommend a special nut grinding mill to mince frozen pieces of beef heart after two or three minutes of thawing. The resultant pieces look a bit like little worms, a shape much preferred by the discus.

Another important live food is whiteworms, but it is much too tedious to breed them. They are bred readily in plastic boxes, but it is too difficult to separate them from their food and breeding substrate to get enough clean worms. For this you may want to try a little trick. The earth with the contained worms is put under a lamp where, due to the heat and dehydrating effect of the light, the earth dries and the worms gather in the middle. As soon as the ball of worms is removed and picked apart, a feeding of pure whiteworms is possible. This feeding is especially important during the spawning season as it will increase vitality when given with an additional feeding of vitamins.

Although young fish may quickly adapt to almost any kind of food, older fish will need much more patience. Do not expect adult fish to

**Not only must discus be healthy, they must not be shy. Photo by the author.**

greedily eat new foods. It may be necessary to remove the food and repeat the feeding several times. It is easier to use a new food if one of the fish likes it, because the other fish become "jealous." Once I had five wild discus that due to this jealousy at once accepted the food of the other discus in the aquarium. They even accepted food tablets, which were eaten greedily. Adapting a fish to eating commercial food tablets is a

Whiteworms are an excellent food for discus but they can be difficult to clean before feeding. By allowing a portion of the worm-containing soil to dry, the worms can be collected in large, clean clumps. Photos by the author.

great help if you have to administer certain types of medications.

As implied above, many discus do not adapt well to commercial diets, preferring live and frozen foods. Because of the convenience of prepared foods, however, it is well to attempt to adapt your fish to tablets and pellets on at least an occasional basis. Your pet shop will have a large selection of foods for you to try. Remember that young fish adapt to new foods better and faster than adults.

Large feedings are not necessary, as normally too much food is offered to the fish anyway. Adult discus have to be fed regularly three or four times a day. Young fish should get less food but more often, up to ten times a day. Each feeding should be small enough that it will be eaten almost immediately. Remember that it is necessary to change the water of young fish often—more food, more mess, more changes.

## Vitamins

There currently is little knowledge concerning the demand for vitamins specifically by aquarium fishes. This is not hard to understand when you remember that even today there are many unsolved problems about the uses and requirements for vitamins by humans. We do know that aquarium fishes need vitamins A, $D_3$, and E, and that a lack of these vitamins may cause problems.

### Vitamin A

Also known as retinol, vitamin A is contained in many plants and is derived from carotene, among other

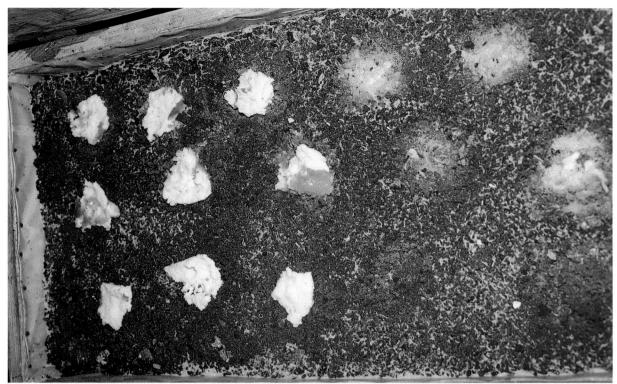

**Whiteworms can be fed on biscuits, bread, and other scraps. A successful colony may smell a bit, but any inconvenience is worthwhile because of the way discus love this food. Photo by the author.**

sources. As discus normally eat mostly meat, they often suffer from a lack of vitamin A that in nature they would get in the intestines of plant-eating prey or from algae and diatoms. Lack of vitamin A leads to poor growth, poor appetite, weak colors, and damage to fins and the liver.

### Vitamin D

Pure vitamin D usually is found in foods in small quantities, but many chemicals that yield vitamin D (provitamins) occur in discus prey. There is no detailed experience concerning deficiencies of vitamin $D_3$ in discus, but small supplements are recommended. Your pet dealer or veterinarian can suggest a practical supplement to be put on or in the food. No problems with overdosing have been noted,

but be cautions and do not over-supplement.

Personally, I think that a $D_3$ supplement is very important for bringing up young fish. It is known that trout have a daily demand of 1500 to 2000 units of vitamin $D_3$ per kilo (2.2 pounds) of body weight, which is given as a supplement in the food. You might try putting a drop of oil-based $D_3$ on a food tablet and feeding the tablet a few hours later when the oil is absorbed. If you wish to add the $D_3$ to dry food or beef heart, a water-soluble supplement should be used. One drop of supplement for two young fish or one adult discus is sufficient.

### Vitamin E

Vitamin E (tocopherol) is especially necessary when breeding, and any food that could influence spawning must contain it. Normally vitamin E (and also vitamins

A, D, and K) is fat-soluble, which means oily. Thus it cannot be used by just dropping it into the water; it has to be added to the food. Soluble vitamin E sometimes is available in pet shops.

A vitamin E supplement can be added to food tablets and allowed to dry; the treated tablets can be kept in the refrigerator for several weeks. After some weeks a reduction of potency is possible, but it really doesn't impair the utility of the vitamin. Another possible application is to put soluble (not oil-based) vitamin E directly into the aquarium, 1 ml to 100 L (26 gallons) of water.

### The B-complex vitamins

Other important vitamins are $B_1$, $B_2$, $B_6$, and $B_{12}$, which influence the metabolism of carbohydrates. The value of these vitamins is known from salmon and haddock

**Adult discus often adapt to eating tablet foods, which is very convenient if you wish to medicate the fish or add vitamin and mineral supplements. Photo by the author.**

especially if they are being fed heavily on brine shrimp nauplii, which may lead to poor growth. Young fish even a few days old should be given vitamin C supplements.

**Feeding young**

If the parent fish quarrel, they should be separated so only one of the pair is looking after the spawn. In such a case you also should feed the young fish brine shrimp nauplii. It is very simple to raise brine shrimp. The following general instructions should always yield to the actual instructions on the eggs you buy at your pet shop. There are many different types of brine shrimp, each with its own temperature requirement, salt concentration, and hatching time. When in doubt, read the instructions.

For each 0.7 L (1.5 pints) of water add the amount of salt suggested by the packager (usually several spoonfuls). Sprinkle on a spoonful of brine shrimp eggs ("cysts") from your pet shop. For best results the water and eggs should be aerated, so if you are using a bottle cork it and lead in the airline tubing through a hole in the cork. If you are hatching the shrimp in a flat pan, aeration is not as necessary, although the swirling effect of the air probably increases hatching success. Keep the water at about 20 to 28°C (68 to 82°F) for 24 to 30 hours (follow package instructions). Larvae can be filtered out for feeding as soon as they are visible (be sure to remove the eggshells— the larvae are attracted to light and can be siphoned off cleanly from in front of the beam). Brine shrimp nauplii

experiments. For instance, poor growth of trout due to lack of vitamin B$_1$ is not uncommon. Necrosis (death and decomposition) of the gills may be due in part to a lack of vitamin B.

**Vitamin C**

The last important vitamin is the soluble vitamin C, ascorbic acid, sold as a powder in pet shops and through veterinarians and fed mixed with beef heart. 500 grams (about 1 pound) of beef

heart can be enriched with one spoonful of vitamin C.

As discus very often show problems in growth, it is essential to pay special attention to vitamin C levels. Lack of this vitamin may result in softening of the bones and damage to the gills, especially in the case of young fish. (Of course, other things may lead to damage of gills, such as lack of hormones, poor genetics, and bacteria.) In any case, young fish should be given additional vitamin C,

You know you are a success when your discus feed from your hand.

Brine shrimp are an essential food for young discus and hatching stations should be part of every fishroom. Photo by the author.

Medicines and vitamin and mineral supplements can be added to food tablets and allowed to dry thoroughly. Photo by the author.

Proper foods and feeding techniques are essential in producing healthy discus. The discus keeper must be constantly aware of not only what his fish are eating, but how enthusiastic they eat it. Commercial frozen foods (such as turkey heart, above), prepared foods (tablets, top right), and live foods (brine shrimp, below) are all satisfactory. Photos by the author.

can be fed to discus only five days old and are an excellent supplement to the mucus from their parents' sides. Feed only as much as the fry will eat, because uneaten nauplii will die and can contaminate the water. By setting up several

**A varied diet is essential for healthy discus. Live foods such as whiteworms (above) can be alternated with commercial foods such as tablets (below). Photos by the author.**

cultures at one- or two-day intervals you will have a continuing source of food.

Tubifex worms should not be fed to discus as they normally contain heavy metals that could lead to poisoning or intestinal problems. The same problems unfortunately may be true of bloodworms that came from contaminated mud.

Once the discus are used to a varied diet in their youth, there will be no problems when they become adults. All my discus will on occasion even take commercial food tablets so I can treat them with medicines and vitamins that must be added to the tablets. Live and frozen foods are of course preferred.

Small discus should be fed several times daily, up to ten times if they are separated from their parents. Such frequent feedings and regular changes of part of the water every day will lead to rapid and healthy growth.

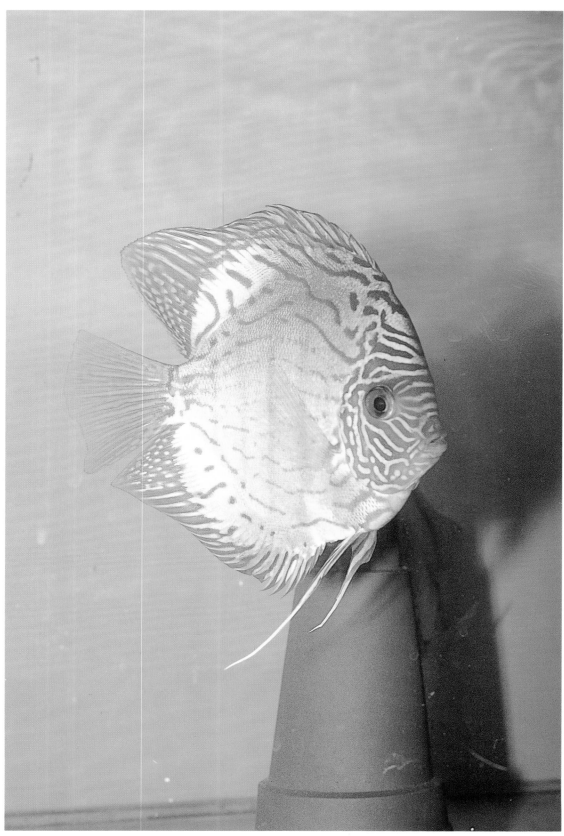

A brilliant turquoise discus with the typical long ventral fins found in adult discus. Photo by the author.

# Breeding discus

## Sex determination

Determining the sex of discus is a problem that cannot be solved easily as discus have no clear external sexual characters. Only during the actual spawning process is it possible to determine their sex with certainty: the male's breeding tube is shorter and more pointed than the female's longer and blunter ovipositor. More experienced discus breeders may be able to distinguish the sexes with some certainty, especially if comparing animals of the same age. This is due to the heavier male skull imparting a broader, more rounded silhouette than that of the

**Living plants highlight this cobalt blue discus. Photo by the author.**

Discus fry only a few hours after hatching are checked by a parent. A few white (probably sterile) eggs can be seen. Photo by the author.

A brilliant turquoise female. Notice the thin upper lip. Photo by the author.

**Almost any type of ceramic pottery of the correct shape and size can be used as a substrate for the eggs. The base should be temporarily but securely anchored so the pot or cone will not topple during spawning. Photo by the author.**

order to choose a good discus pair.

If you have chosen a good pair, you will see it in their behavior: they no longer attack each other but eat calmly together and no longer push each other. These characters are very important in obtaining a good spawning. Normally the female discus is pushed around by the male when they are not spawning. He keeps her in a corner except during feeding and changes his behavior only during spawning, when the female becomes an equal partner. After spawning they both look after the eggs and the fry equally.

**Selection of breeding discus**

The different varieties of discus can be crossbred, which means that breeding of different strains will introduce certain markings into the new discus line. Crossbreeding of some varieties may lead to a type of inbreeding showing the required markings, but the aim should be breeding of varieties that will maintain the required varietal characters for a long time.

When selecting adult discus it is very easy to compare colors, fins, and shape of body. The selection should also consider the sex, at least making an educated guess. The female discus is a little smaller than the male and the tips of her fins are a bit more rounded. The discus selected should be kept together in an aquarium to give them a chance to form pairs. They should be given at least two spawning cones or similar spawning substrates.

Another possibility would be to choose ten young discus

female, if the two are viewed together. Thicker lips also seem to be a male characteristic, as are longer filaments on the ventral fins. A broader tail fin may be a male characteristic. The behavior of the fish in the aquarium may indicate their sex, but smaller female discus may be more dominant than their mates. Very often the female discus have stronger vertical bars than the males.

It is necessary to study the fish over a long period to determine their sex through a combination of the external characters and behavior in from one breeding and raise them with similar specimens from a second breeding of the desired type. However, this would require much more time as a discus needs approximately one year to become fully adult. After half a year you will be able to select the ten or 12 best discus to raise to adulthood for breeding. With luck they will form pairs among themselves.

You could try the same technique with adult discus, but you would have more problems with fighting. There also is less chance that you will be lucky and get an actual mated pair by mixing adults. Changing mates in mated pairs may not work. Thus, offering a new male to an adult female may lead to trouble. It also may happen that the forced pair will not spawn, although they got along well for a time, or they might eat the eggs. There is no way to force a spawning.

**Egg-eating**

Normally pairs live together peacefully, even when not spawning. Although they remain paired, it is possible that they will occasionally quarrel, which is a very important problem when spawning is taking place. Quarreling fish may eat their eggs. Some discus are notorious egg-eaters. Normally such fish cannot be used for further breeding. This is a very old problem, and no one really knows its cause. It seems not to be hunger. Perhaps too many or too few breeding activities? Quarrels? The wrong water? Nobody knows.

My suggestion is to not look for the reasons, but look after the eggs. The eggs must be

protected. Wire netting of 5 to 6 mm (a fifth to a quarter of an inch) mesh should be put around the spawn at a distance of about one centimeter (half an inch) so the parents can see their eggs but cannot eat them. The netting should be kept up until the fry become free-swimming because this may increase the instincts of the parents.

This method also can be helpful in "re-educating" some fish that are bad egg-eaters. It is used regularly in Asia.

This proven pair of excellent discus exemplifies the difficulties of distinguishing the sexes. The male (in the foreground) is virtually identical to the female. Even experts have trouble sexing discus. Photo by the author.

A breeding pair of German red turquoise discus with their eggs. Photo by the author.

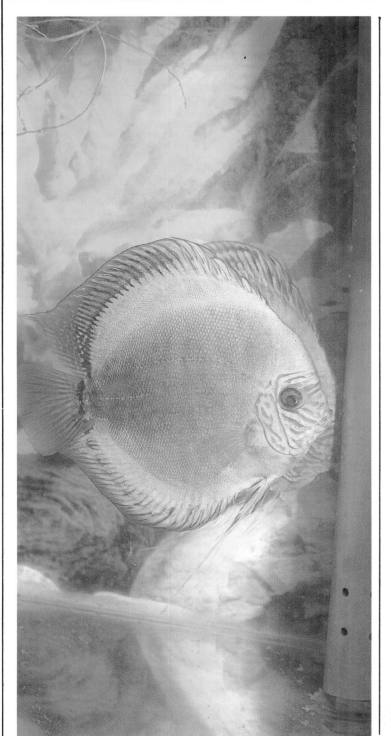
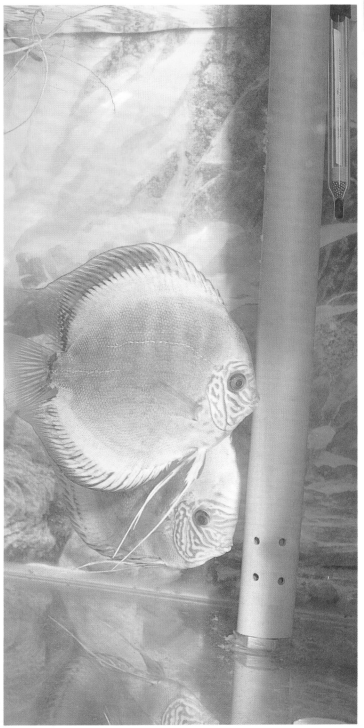

If not presented with a suitable spawning substrate, discus will find their own. This pair of gorgeous cobalt blues spawned on a plastic filter pipe. The only problem with this is that the eggs are harder to control as the spawning substrate cannot be moved and is difficult to surround by wire mesh if the parents look like they might eat the eggs. It is much better to make sure that suitable spawning cones are always available to potential spawning pairs. Photos by the author.

Above: A group of adult brilliant turquoise discus. If kept together, adult discus often pair naturally. Photo by the author.

Left: Fry feeding on the side of a Heckel discus, *Symphysodon discus*, a species seldom kept and bred in pure form. Photo by the author.

Right: A pair of wild Heckel discus covered with their fry. This species seldom spawns successfully in captivity and is seldom available on the market. Photo by the author.

Below: A male turquoise discus. This specimen has a distinctly heavy head and relatively pointed fins. Photo by the author.

Discus hatchlings are not round like the parents but more elongated like typical cichlids (below). The shape gradually changes (top left) until, at six weeks, the young are similar to the parents in general appearance (top right). Photos by the author.

**These one-week-old fry are dependent on their parents for both protection and the proper food in the form of mucus from the sides. The mucus is essential to the growth of young discus and is virtually impossible to successfully duplicate. Photo by the author.**

Left: Long-finned discus have recently been produced. The author is attempting to concentrate red colors into the elongated area to highlight the lengthened finnage. Photo by the author.

Below: A difficult crossing between a wild brown female and a cultivated turquoise male. Wild adults are difficult to acclimate and breed. Photo by the author.

## Spawning

Once a breeding pair is formed they can be expected to spawn. Their colors get much darker above. The vertical stripes become much darker and clearer but will disappear later on so that only the stripe through the eye can be seen.

The discus start spawning by shaking the spawning cone and cleaning it. The sexual tube (ovipositor) of the female may be seen as it is about 3 to 4 mm (1/8 to 1/6 inch) long and longer than that of the male. After several "trials" the female starts depositing the eggs in regular rows. The male immediately fertilizes them. Normally a spawning results in about 150 to 200 eggs, although up to 500 eggs are possible.

The spawning process itself lasts approximately one hour, and the synchronization of the couple is fantastic. After spawning, the parents stay in front of the eggs, fanning them with their fins.

During incubation the fish should be fed. Great care should be taken that the water remains clean. Because the appetite is reduced now, there is more of a chance of excess food being overlooked in the water or on the bottom. Keep the water clean!

Normal discus eggs are clear when first laid and will hatch after about 60 hours. This time may be reduced if the water is 30° to 32°C (86–90°F). After another 50 to 60 hours the larvae begin to swim. A successful breeding is possible only if the young fish are able to find and feed from the skin of the parents. If not, they soon die.

For the first few days the young discus live only on the mucus from the parents' skin.

These fish, the offspring of a cross between a Heckel discus and a turquoise, still show the accentuated midbody vertical band of the Heckel parent. Photo by the author.

A pair of brown discus with their young. Photo by the author.

**Above: By four months of age the excellent shape of a Degen discus is obvious. Photo by the author. Below: Yellow eyes are unpopular in Europe, so breeders must pay attention to eye color. Photo by the author.**

**Above: Young discus old enough to begin eating brine shrimp. Photo by the author. Below: It was difficult to get young from this mixed pair of red turquoise female and blue male. Photo by the author.**

A red turquoise female begins laying eggs on a spawning cone. The male must be present to fertilize the eggs within minutes of laying or the sperm will not be able to penetrate the egg membrane. Photo by the author.

They soon accept brine shrimp nauplii and even additional feedings of commercial fry food. At the age of four weeks they will be some 15 mm (0.6 inch) and can be moved to a separate tank. At the age of six to eight weeks they may be over 25 mm (1 inch) and can be sold.

### Breeding tips

First of all you should pay attention to the aquarium itself. It should be at least 1 m (3 feet) from the ground, but I always prefer to raise it another 30 cm (1 foot) because — due to the lighting — the fish are not as frightened or shy. As discus are very "friendly," they should always be quiet, curious, and awaiting their owner.

Another factor is the lighting system. As the breeding aquarium normally contains no plants, the lighting may be weaker than for a planted aquarium. A "warm" full-spectrum light should be used. During spawning a light should burn all night. Approximately 15 watts will be sufficient. Because discus really sleep at night, they will be found quietly resting on the bottom of the tank in the morning. You shouldn't feed them immediately as they will not accept any food until they are fully awake. It is best to wait another half an hour.

The filtering system should be turned off once spawning has started but for no longer than an hour. The flowing water may prevent the fertilization of the eggs.

A further important factor is the spawning cone, which should be at least 20 to 25 cm (8–10 inches) in height. If it doesn't stand firmly on the

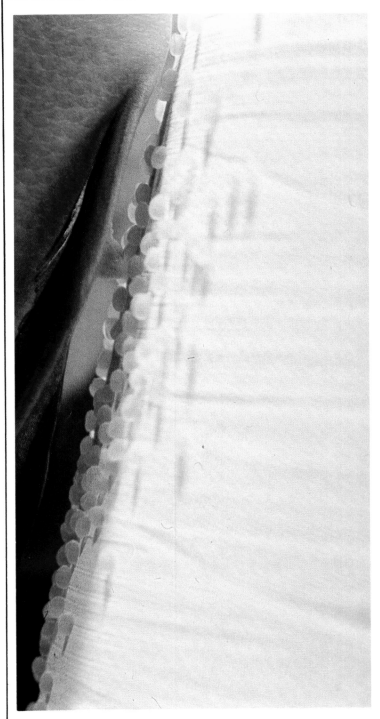

In this close-up of a laying female, the ovipositor can be seen. This is the only certain way of distinguishing the sexes in discus—if you see a fish lay eggs, it is a female; if it fertilizes eggs, it is a male. Photo by the author, Musstopf.

Some female discus have unusual ideas of where to lay their eggs. This particular female chose a foam filter as the spawning site, a poor spot indeed. Photo by the author.

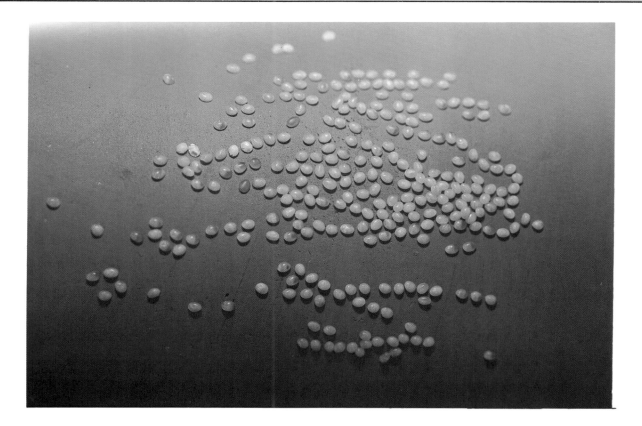

Above: This entire clutch of eggs was rendered sterile by the wrong pH of the tank water. Very soft water also is a necessity for successfully spawning discus. Photo by the author.

Left: Because many discus parents have a tendency to eat some or all their eggs, it is best to cover any spawn with wire mesh. This keeps the parents from snacking and allows the fry to leave to feed on the parental mucus. Photo by the author.

As a rule, discus are good parents, carefully guarding the eggs and keeping them aerated. For unknown reasons, however, almost any discus can turn into an egg-eater, so forethought by the breeder is required to prevent problems. Photo by the author.

Successful breeding operations require tank space. It is not uncommon to have 100 or more young discus survive a single spawning, and they must be raised to either salable size or adulthood if you wish to select the best specimens for breeding. Usually the sizes are segregated to prevent problems, but discus generally are peaceful fish. At top left, the author with one of his 2 meters (6 feet) rearing tanks. Photos by the author.

**Although discus eggs can be raised without the presence of the parents, it is much easier and more efficient to leave the parent with the eggs. This male is guarding the spawn against not only large predators but also against fungus and micropredators. Photo by the author.**

ground, it should be anchored by silicone rubber on a base that can be removed later.

An additional aid to increase breeding success is to change the temperature of the water by about two degrees either cooler or warmer. It's also possible to patiently change the pH value a bit with a few drops of phosphoric acid or peat extract.

If the parent discus do not produce enough mucus, you can increase the amount by using tablets of a drug called Yohimbin, one tablet per 100 L (26 gallons) of water. This mixture is put into the water one day before the young fish become free-swimming. The drug promotes mucus production. A harmful side-effect is that the discus may not spawn again for a long time after having been in this mixture, but if you are able to save the present brood it may be worth it. The decision is yours.

A common problem is fungused eggs. This may happen for several reasons. One of the least likely reasons is that the male discus is infertile and cannot fertilize the eggs. By keeping records of spawning success with individual fish you will be able to determine if the male should be replaced.

The main reason for fungusing is that the sperm cannot successfully penetrate into the eggs. Our problem is reflected in a similar problem found in trout breeding. In large trout hatcheries millions of eggs are fertilized artificially. The semen (milt) is removed from the male and placed with the eggs in a process called *dry fertilization*. This is because sperm have very short lives in the water. If

**Above: These discus have spawned successfully twice in just two weeks. Small fry from their first spawning can be seen on the adults's sides, while eggs and nearly hatched fry can be seen on and at the base of the cone. Photo by the author. Below: Most of the eggs in this clutch are white, indicating they were sterile and have become fungused. Photo by the author.**

the eggs float in the water the membrane seals after about two minutes so that no sperm may enter. This results in unfertilized eggs subject to fungus infection. Thus it is possible to outsmart nature by stopping the filtering system during the spawning process.

Discus eggs will need about 65 hours at 28°C (82°F), 55 hours at 31°C (88°F), and 72 hours at 25°C (77°F). However, in case of temperatures higher than 29°C (86°F) fungus is very possible owing to germination of mold spores in the water. As mold spores are found normally in the water, they should be killed before spawning commences. Malachite green can be used to treat the water and also to bathe the fertilized eggs. Fungicides are sold in your pet shop. Fungicides can be added immediately after spawning and should be stopped after 12 to 18 hours. If the degree of fungus infection continues to increase, the medication can be given until the beginning of the second day. It may not be put into the water later than this as it would damage the parents' skin.

Another problem could be too much salt in the water. Because the membrane of the discus egg is porous, fluid leaves the egg through osmosis, resulting in the egg shrinking and failing. If you see clear eggs on the

**Facing page: This rather perverse female has spawned on the glass, ignoring the spawning cone supplied. Notice the fine mesh covering the filter tubes, a precaution to keep fry from being carried away. Photo by the author.**

spawning cone and they do not develop further but also do not develop fungus, the defect possibly is due to salty water. A change with desalted water is necessary.

In the meantime there also are sold reversible systems on the market that are very helpful because the water remains completely unsalty and sterile!

**To be on the safe side, it is is best to cover all spawnings with wire mesh. Although the parents will still be able to see and guard the eggs, it does prevent those heartbreaking occurrences when one or both parents eat the eggs. The fry must be able to get to the mucus on the parents's sides, however. Photo by the author.**

Facing page: The obvious "saddle" or concavity on the nose of this discus is a major fault that must be eliminated from the line. Such faulty fish must not be allowed to breed. Careful culling of young discus is essential to prevent objectionable adults. Photo by the author.

Left: A tankful of excellent young Degen discus all the same size and shape. Uniformly fine young produce fine adults. Photo by the author.

At just two weeks of age, these brown young are already eating tablet food. Photo by the author.

## Surprises in breeding

In summary, a normal spawning sequence starts with the cleaning of the spawning cone. The spawning tube of the female discus can be clearly seen. Many yellow eggs then are laid on the cone. The male discus fertilizes them immediately. The spawning process lasts about one hour. The parents normally rest beside their spawn. Depending on the temperature of the water, after 36 hours you may already see dark contents within the eggs. Sixty hours later there will be larvae in the eggs, and in another 60 hours the fry will have hatched. They stay on the cone but may be moved about by their parents to another place. Feeding on the parents' skin mucus now occurs. After four to six days, feeding with brine shrimp nauplii can begin. After another three to four weeks the young fish can be separated from their parents. At least, that's the way things usually go. Many problems may arise, however.

It may happen that after one set of eggs is laid another spawning may be added to the cone. In this case, the parents normally look after the first batch of eggs, but as soon as the fry start to swim they no longer look after the fry but concentrate on the second batch of eggs. These young fish now are without help, and if they rest on the bodies of the parents they are brushed off. The eggs are always more important to the parents.

Once I caught some fry in a

**A major disaster in any breeding program is the loss of a batch of fry because the parents are unable to produce enough skin mucus to feed the young. Although rare, this problem is occasionally encountered. Photo by the author.**

Fry and young fish are instinctively attracted to the parents both as a source of food and for protection. Cichlids in general have very strong family bonds, often with special parental behaviors that draw the fish to them in emergencies. There also is evidence that some other cichlids (such as *Etroplus* and *Uaru*) may produce a form of skin mucus to supplement the feeding of their young. Photo by the author.

**Left:** By the time they are a few weeks old, the cloud of young discus begins to disperse to search for food. These fish will readily accept live foods and prepared foods from this point on. Photo by the author.

This inbred male comes from wild green discus parents. Notice the distinct filament on the soft rays of the dorsal fin, a feature not found in every adult discus. Photo by the author.

slender tube and put them into another aquarium, attempting to get the discus pair there to accept the "new" fish. When the fry tried to get on the bodies of the foster parents, they were accepted. The foster parents looked after 120 of their own and 40 other young.

Another time, there was a spawning during my absence. My son looked after them and took many photos of the spawning. Once there were fry on their bodies, the pair had another spawning, so they had a lot of fry on the body and also lots of new eggs on the cone. As I was absent, I couldn't remove the cone. Of course, only a part of the 40 fry developing from the second spawning could fit on the parents' bodies, but the parents made no distinction between the young of the two broods and I had no problems.

Of course, it also is possible to change the spawning or even young fish and put them with other parents. Even highly bred discus may not look after the spawning or may eat their eggs regularly. It is not necessary to put the eggs in water when moving them to another aquarium. Color of the adult makes no difference: it is possible to exchange the eggs of a brown and a turquoise pair. I once put the spawning cone of a brown pair next to the cone of a turquoise pair, and the turquoise discus looked after both spawnings and did not distinguish their offspring from those of the brown ones. The young fish grew up in an aquarium of 360 L (94 gallons) and reached a size of about 6 cm (2 1/2 inches) before I could clearly distinguish them.

A large number of young fish means a large amount of food. Large amounts of food mean large amounts of wastes. Large amounts of wastes mean regular water changes and great care in maintaining the proper pH and water chemistry. Discus are sensitive fish, and young discus are even more sensitive than adults. Regular and consistent tank maintenance is the key to success. Photos by the author.

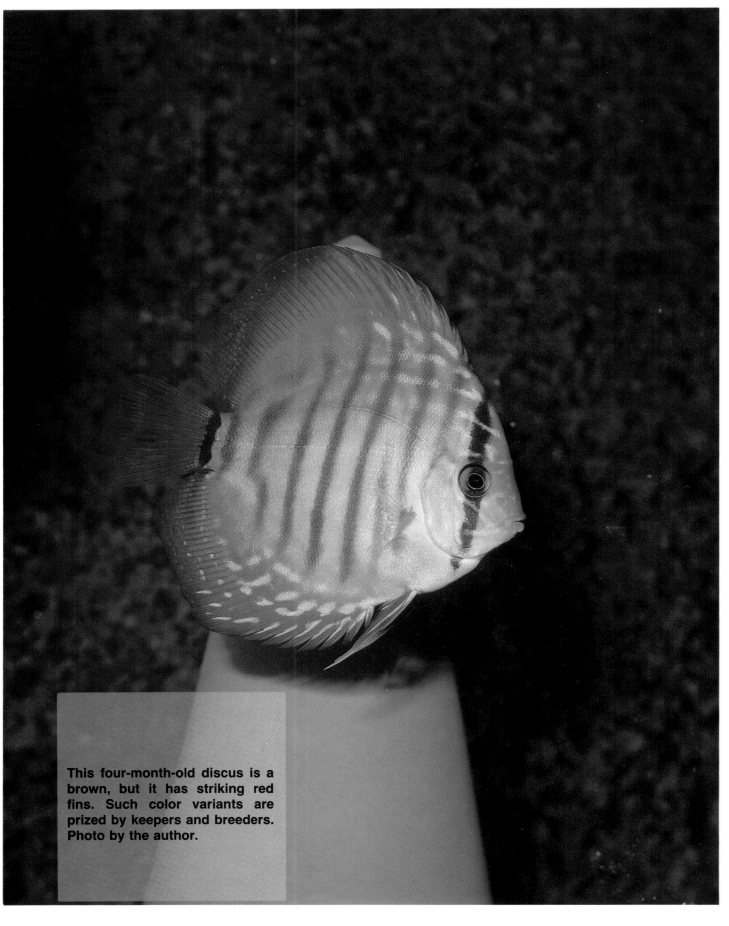

This four-month-old discus is a brown, but it has striking red fins. Such color variants are prized by keepers and breeders. Photo by the author.

**Above: This four-month-old fish has not developed correctly. The shape is not round enough and the eye is relatively too large. Photo by the author. Below: A very interesting female bred from wild brown and green parents. Photo by the author.**

It is possible to put new eggs with any pair while their own eggs are already several hours old. Thus it may happen that the "new" parents would be waiting up to 100 hours for all the eggs to hatch. On the other hand, "new" parents are not "surprised" if they get larvae after just 12 hours.

Once I had a pair that spawned regularly every four days — on the cone, on the filter, on the heater — without looking after their eggs. Sometimes I was able to collect the eggs and put them with another pair. When I put another pair into this 1 m (3-foot) aquarium of 250 L (65 gallons), the "old" parents looked after their eggs because now there were fish in the water that seemed to be enemies.

### Discus milk

During the first days and weeks the young discus feed on mucus on the parents' sides, the so-called discus milk. They do not stop feeding on this milk even if they are fed additionally on brine shrimp or copepod larvae.

For a long time attempts have been made to raise young discus artificially, without their parents, and partial success has been achieved, especially by the American breeder Jack Wattley. However, their growth is poor. With the aid of

**Facing page: Although many eggs in this clutch were infertile and became fungused, many hatched and produced viable young. Photo by the author.**

**A foam filter serves as a substrate for thriving colonies of microscopic plants and animals. These young discus have discovered a wonderful food source and are grazing contentedly. Photo by the author.**

an electron microscope, Dr. Bremer and Dr. Walter made studies on discus milk to determine its structure.

During the breeding process cells called secretocytes are formed on the parents' sides. These are not found on any other fishes. The secretion — the "milk" — is a combination of algae and a number of bacteria with fats and proteins. The young fish live completely from this food, and the bacteria are important in digestion. This essential food of the young discus is not just skin slime, but is a real milk secretion that not only

functions in feeding but also transfers immunity similarly to the mother's milk of mammals.

Therefore, from the studies of Bremer and Walter, it appears to be essential that the young fish feed on the parents' milk for several days. An artificial food cannot replace the parents' milk and is not appreciated by the young.

The secretion of the milk is influenced by circumstances but is best if the parents are well-fed and there is no physical stress as from catching them, frightening them, or handling them too often in the aquarium.

An ideal combination for optimal growth of the young fish is primarily milk feeding with additional feedings of brine shrimp nauplii, copepod larvae, other meaty foods, and some algae. During this time special care should be taken to maintain the quality of the water owing to increased metabolism of the fish and thus more wastes.

**Carotene coloring**

Fish sold as "red discus" or "red turquoise discus" are often seen, but they do not satisfy their purchasers for long because their colors get weaker and weaker. This is because their bright colors are due to special foods, not genetics.

Natural red colors due to food are not uncommon. For example, trout have a red lateral stripe that shines brightly during spawning. If breeding trout are fed on a natural food such as crustaceans with a high carotene content, their flesh becomes redder instead of the normal pale color. The carotene leads to an increase in red color of the skin and the meat.

Experiments with trout show that those fed additionally with 48 g (1.7 ounces) of canthacanthin per kg (2.2 pounds) had a redder meat and external color after several months. (Canthacanthin yields carotene.) Approximately eight weeks after the special feeding stopped, the coloring of the flesh was diminished by 50%, as also was the coloring of the lateral stripe and the gills.

It is very simple to feed

About 60 hours after hatching, the fry are free-swimming and able to attach to the sides of the parents to begin feeding on the special mucus. Photo by the author.

discus with extra carotene by feeding them more shrimp and other crustaceans and ground crustacean shells. This special feeding has long been used in Thailand, Taiwan, Singapore, and Japan, where carotene feeding is used to achieve a strong red coloring. The best effect can be seen on discus babies fed with brine shrimp, as long as the feeding continues. A change in feeding, as to beef heart, means a loss of the red color. Fairness requires that the customer be told that the discus have been fed a special color food.

All insiders know that artificial coloring of discus is possible, but for me the problem is that such a coloring evidently is encouraged by the demands of the marketplace. This could lead to breeding of pale discus that at a size of 3 to 4 cm (1-1.5 inches) have brilliant colors unlike natural colors. Well-known merchants and breeders do not artificially color their fish, as the intensity in color will weaken after just a few weeks or months because it is based only on feedings or hormones.

In addition to carotene foods, artificial colors can be produced by hormones. It is possible to get "electric-blue" turquoise discus within 48 hours and to get Heckel discus with bright blue heads. From simple green discus, royal greens can be produced with hormones.

Because it is very difficult to inject many small discus, it is normal to treat their water with sex hormones such as estrogen and androgen. The hormone androgen will increase the aggressiveness of the fish as well as intensity of colors. Testosterone is the

usual source of androgen.

One tablet of this hormone in an aquarium of 100 L (26 gallons) achieves a change in color after 48 hours, but there is much conjecture about whether the fish will be damaged either physically or through failures of the reproductive systems. For this reason I cannot accept any change in coloring due to hormones and prefer to go back to standard breeding of fancy lines based on genetics.

We do not really need all the fantastic names. Many breeders like to keep such

**This colorful breeding pair of discus was produced by a Hong Kong breeder. Although the quality of some Asian discus is too low for serious breeders to consider, others are excellent fish that adapt well to aquarium conditions.**

names as "cobalt blue" or "scarlet red" because of increased marketing strength. As you do not actually know the final development of the young discus, it is necessary that the parents have healthy bodies and good, clear colors. Normally, if the parents are beautiful fish, their descendants also will be beautiful discus.

The blossoming of German discus breeding began in 1960, and since 1970 the number of discus breeders has been increasing, partly due to the considerable breeding success now available to anyone. The most important varieties now are the several types of turquoise discus like those bred in the United States and Asia.

The two major breeders of German discus: Dr. Eduard Schmidt-Focke at the left and the author, Bernd Degen, at the right. Dr. Schmidt-Focke was the first important German discus breeder and produced fish that were the foundation stock of the modern German discus. Photo by Dr. H. R. Axelrod.

### Discus breeding in Germany

German discus breeders began to raise discus in large numbers about the same time that, in the United States, Jack Wattley had the first success with his turquoise discus. In Germany, Dr. Eduard Schmidt-Focke was the first important discus breeder. He had enormous success with his crossbreedings, which are now the basis of German fancy discus breeding.

### Turquoise Discus

High in the popularity stakes. Light turquoise, with even line markings over the body, the background color brown. Also offered with plain light turquoise bodies, but not considered of top quality. Terms such as "electric blue," "peppermint green," "high-finned," "cobalt blue," and "royal green" are actually marketing names and not the names of distinct varieties.

### Brilliant Turquoise Discus

Has a very electric-blue color of the horizontal lines over the whole body. The dark background color is seen only between the lines.

### All-Turquoise Discus

Has a very intense color over the whole body with no visible areas of brown background color. Distinct lines can only be found on the head. The color is a deep turquoise or pale blue without vertical bars. This color is very heavily dependent upon the lighting.

### Red-Turquoise Discus

The most beautiful variety, with a deep red background color over the entire body and electric-blue lines. This variety is not bred very often and most discus offered under the name are just brown types. Highly bred red-turquoise discus are very seldom seen.

Fantastic names often are used for reasons of attracting a better market, but they are not acceptable by better dealers. To ensure distinctive genetic lines only healthy and beautiful discus should be used for breeding. It is not unheard of for "ordinary" discus to produce young with turquoise markings. A guarantee cannot be given as many young fish will have turquoise markings that will disappear later.

German discus breeders have to pay special attention to their water, as the tap water is too hard and the nitrates and other contaminants are steadily increasing so that ion exchangers always are necessary.

Some breeders with large numbers of young fish are

Above: An excellent and very consistent group of German red turquoise discus. Such fish are sought by many aquarists and breeders. Photo by the author. Below: Large, properly lighted and planted display tanks make excellent room decorations.

No matter how beautiful the body and fin colors or attractive the shape, the poor eye color of this specimen ruins it for consideration as a breeder, at least in the minds of many aquarists. The bright red eye is a requirement for a good discus. Photo by the author.

**In the proper light the turquoise discus truly glistens with color. Photo by the author.**

A truly magnificent discus. This is about as large as the species gets in captivity. Photo by the author.

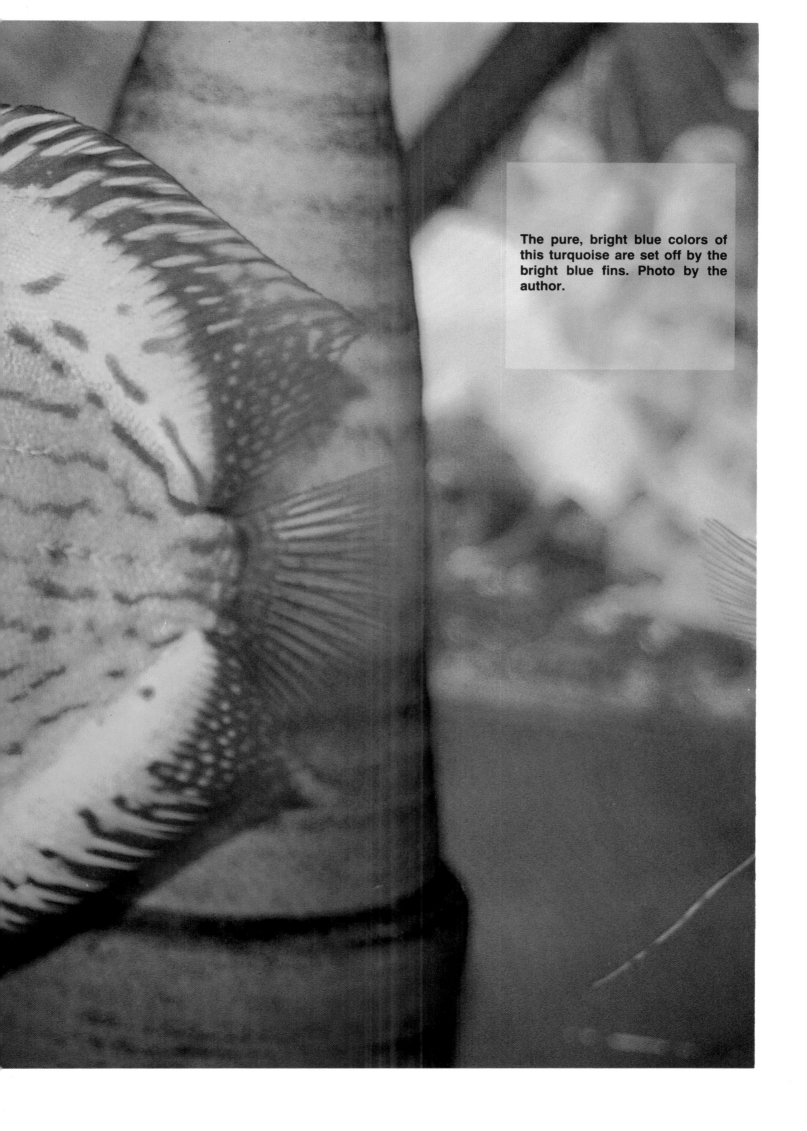

The pure, bright blue colors of this turquoise are set off by the bright blue fins. Photo by the author.

A group of one-year-old German turquoise discus. Few breeders can produce such consistency in shape and color. Photo by the author.

A majestic male discus. Adult discus are among the largest of the commonly kept aquarium fishes and are certainly one of the most colorful. Photo by the author.

In poor light the colors of a discus may be very subdued, with bright blue or green appearing yellowish or even brown. Photo by the author.

**Above: Part of the discus showroom of a German dealer. Here the discus are a bit crowded, but they are displayed in excellent surroundings with good lighting and clean water. Photo by the author.**

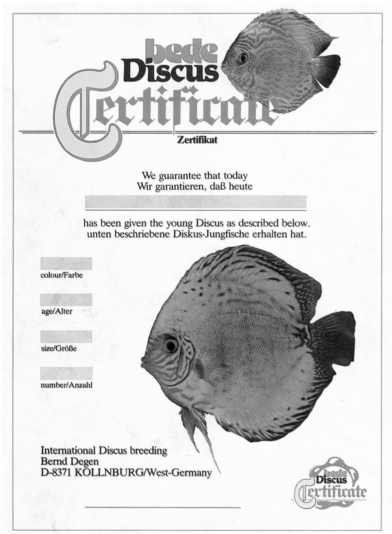

**bede Discus Certificate**

Zertifikat

We guarantee that today
Wir garantieren, daß heute

has been given the young Discus as described below.
unten beschriebene Diskus-Jungfische erhalten hat.

colour/Farbe

age/Alter

size/Größe

number/Anzahl

International Discus breeding
Bernd Degen
D-8371 KÖLLNBURG/West-Germany

**bede Discus Certificate**

**A certificate of authenticity that accompanies Degen discus. Because of the great time and effort required in producing the very best discus, it does not seem unreasonable to give the customer proof of the quality of his investment.**

able to supply young to dealers, and smaller quantities are sold privately.

Many German breeders look for good quality discus, but new breeders often are negligent in making their selections, and the quality of their breeding pairs may not be the highest. In Germany, wild-caught discus are very rare and play a minor part on the market. By introducing colorful wild-caught discus into the breedings, however, they may produce interesting colors. As a whole, it seems that German discus are of a good quality standard.

**The shape of a discus is as important as its color. This brilliant turquoise is higher than normal and thus not the best specimen. Photo by the author.**

## Discus breeding in Asia

The Asian countries are the main producers of discus, especially the aquarium-fish breeders of Hong Kong, Thailand, Singapore, and Malaysia. The tropical climate, the cheap and abundant living foods, and the cheap labor allow Asian breeders to produce attractive discus at low prices. There are some real "breeding factories" specializing in discus and discus breeding.

**This equally colorful male has an excellent round shape that is desired by knowledgeable discus fanciers. Photo by the author.**

A truly spectacular discus, the culmination of the breeder's art. Such fish are seldom seen in local pet shops and are one-of-a-kind items. Photo by the author.

Although this is a wild-taken Heckel discus, the colors are still exceptionally vivid. This fish would be of interest to any serious fancier. Photo by the author.

**Above: A turquoise discus with a spectacular red dorsal fin. Contrast this natural red pattern with the unusual red of the discus below. The bottom discus has been fed on shrimp to produce the red color. Photos by the author.**

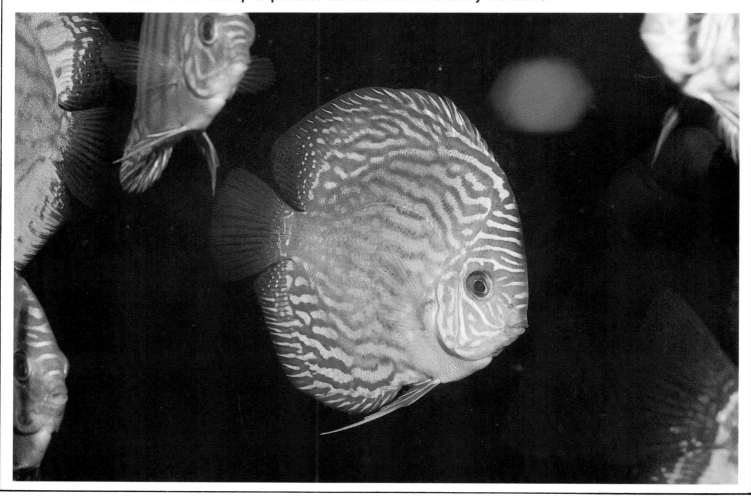

The author visiting a fish exporter in Taiwan.

Cultivated discus bred from wild green Tefe discus. Notice the red spotting on the chest and sides. Photo by the author.

Several years ago, Asia exported mainly brown discus colored by carotene foods to produce deep red markings. Many discus fanciers bought these beautiful red discus and found they had normal brown discus after a few weeks of normal feeding

However, over the years the Asian fish got better and better. Highly bred discus were exported to Asian breeders from Germany. They now are the basis of the Asian discus industry and are of high quality and beautiful appearance. Logically, their descendants should also be as good, but there are some negative influences. For example, the young fish are specially colored by feeding with hormones. At an age of only about four to six weeks the young discus have beautiful colors (instead of waiting months for the color), but damage from the hormones and stress from shipping, changes in water

**Because this pair of discus has been fighting, they have been separated by wire mesh. The mesh is large enough that the young can swim through to be with either parent. Photo by the author.**

**Part of a Japanese fish store where discus are sold. Notice how the tanks are almost bare. The overhead lights probably don't show off the colors to their best. Photo by the author.**

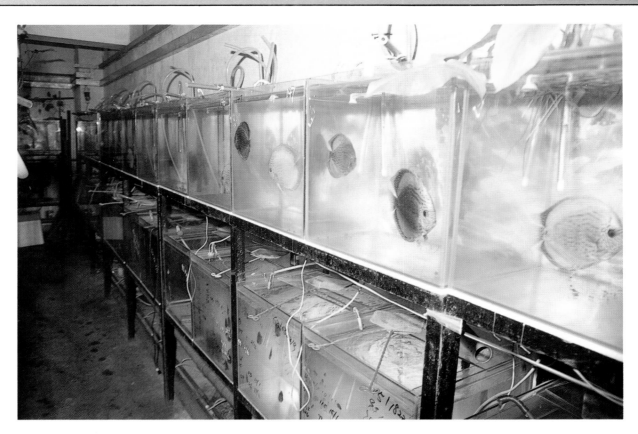

The Orient is able to produce discus and other tropical fishes cheaply because, among other things, the climate is warm enough that the fish can be kept outdoors all year—no heating bills have to be paid. Live foods are cheap and readily available, and labor is cheap. Photos by the author.

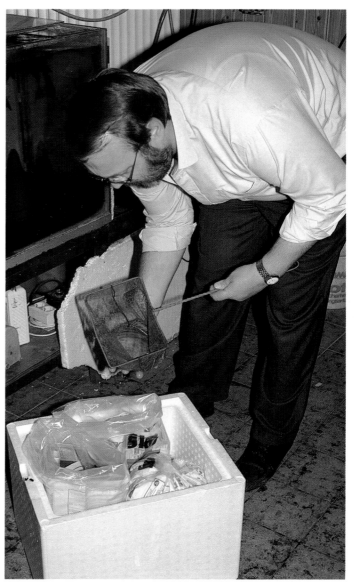

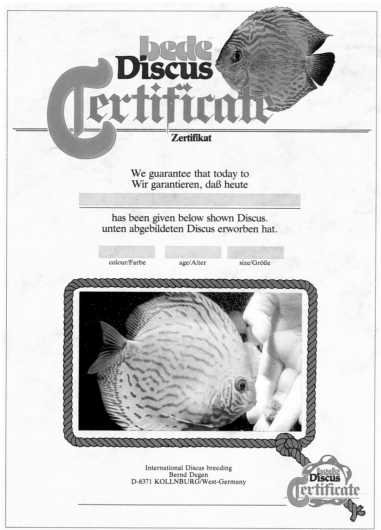

Producing and shipping the best discus in the world is not always an easy task! Every step, from selection of the best breeders and raising of the young to packaging and following through on sales, requires constant attention and a tremendous amount of time. Raising Degen discus is a very labor-intensive effort, but when the certificate is finally made out, it is all worthwhile. Photos by the author.

After each fish is carefully selected by hand, it is individually bagged and packaged in tall, heavy-duty insulated boxes for shipment. Because of a discus's unusual shape and delicate nature, incorrect shipping can ruin a good fish. High packing and shipping costs add significantly to the price of a good discus, but these are essential steps in marketing. Photos by the author.

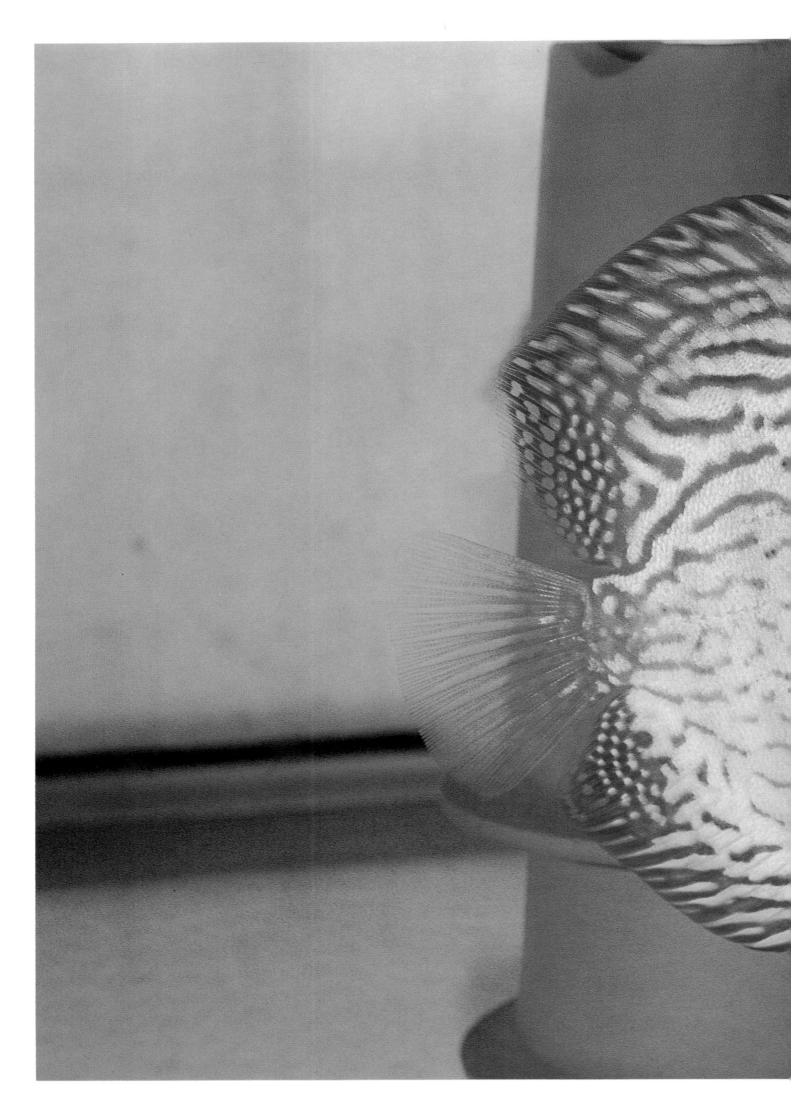

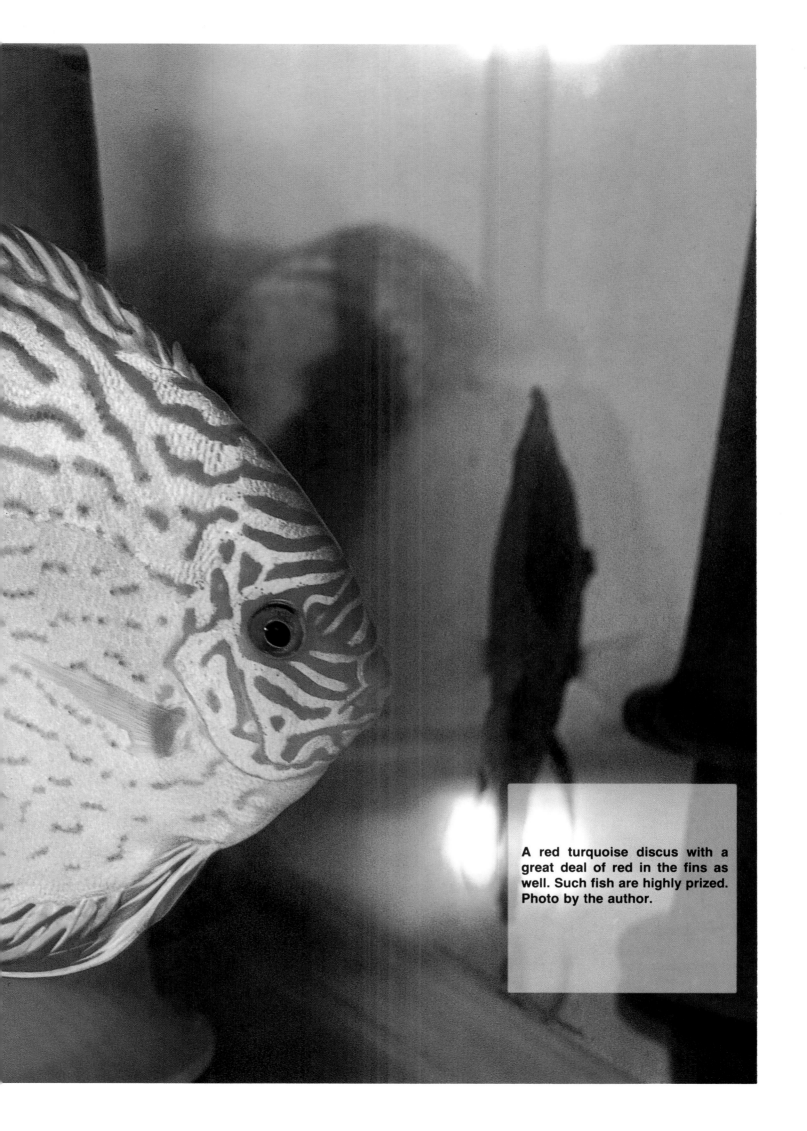

A red turquoise discus with a great deal of red in the fins as well. Such fish are highly prized. Photo by the author.

Although many discus have one or two short filaments at the angle of the dorsal fin, a new mutation developed in Thailand has most of the soft dorsal fin rays elongated. Although found in several colors, this new variant is seldom seen in aquaria and its popularity is not assured. Photos by the author.

chemistry, and changes of food are very heavy, so that imported discus often are not healthy. Their strong colors also get weaker after several weeks. The demand for these fish is very great because of their strong colors and their low prices.

In Asia, the discus are separated by a wire mesh and are put together only for spawning. As a rule, the eggs are secured by another wire net so that their parents cannot eat their eggs, but in this way the parents also have no contact with their young, which are fed on a replacement food.

A hobbyist cannot begin to imagine the number of discus bred for the market. Mass production is necessary, and reduced quality is the logical consequence of mass breedings.

Above: A close-up view of the elongated dorsal rays of the Thai long-finned discus. Photo by the author.

Below: Part of a commercial discus-breeding enterprise in Bangkok. Notice the barren tanks and relatively crowded conditions. Photo by the author.

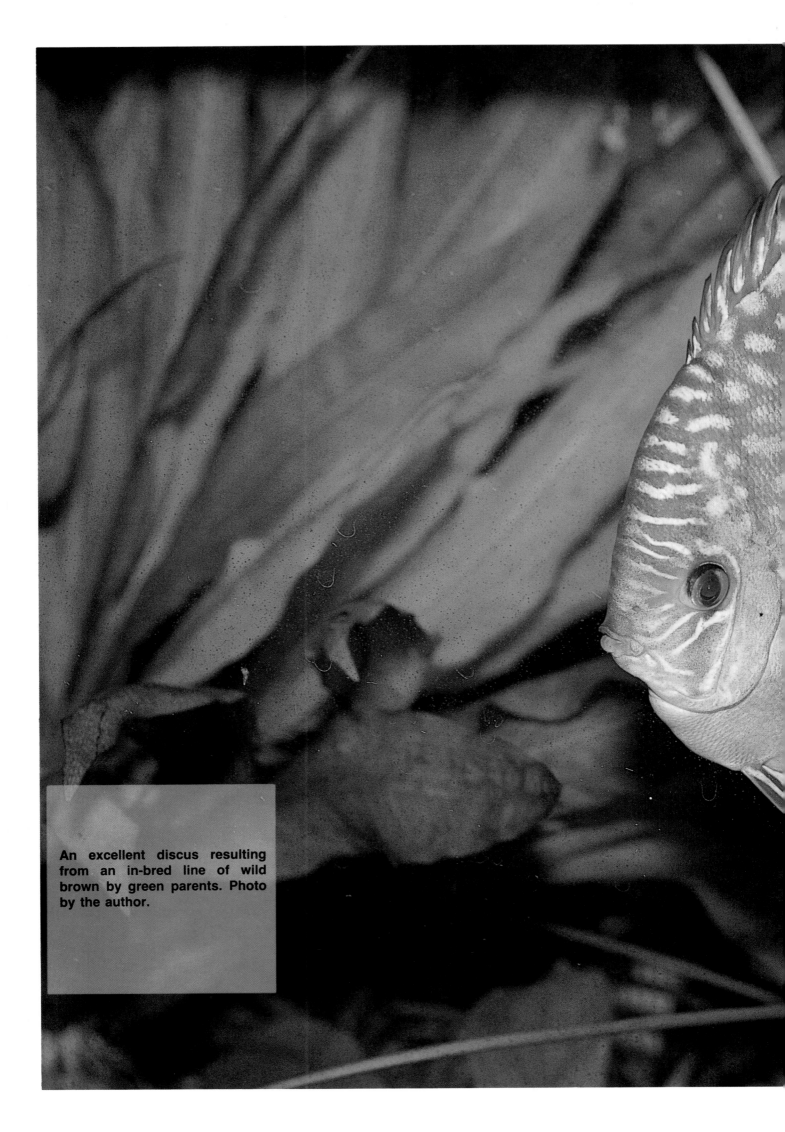

An excellent discus resulting from an in-bred line of wild brown by green parents. Photo by the author.

A Thai breeder counts his fish being prepared for export. Photo by the author.

The author visiting the breeding quarters of Star Aquarium in Bangkok. Photo by the author.

# Illnesses

## General medications

"Illness" is a very serious topic that must be considered at all times. The following list includes many of the drugs that have proved at least somewhat effective when dealing with diseases and problems in some type of fish, not necessarily discus. Whether all are safe and effective with discus is unknown, so consider the following list as being for information only. Discuss all medications with your pet dealer and veterinarian before attempting to treat your fish.

The whitish appearance of the skin mucus of this discus is one of the first symptoms of the mysterious new discus disease. Such fish should be isolated and treated immediately. Photo by the author.

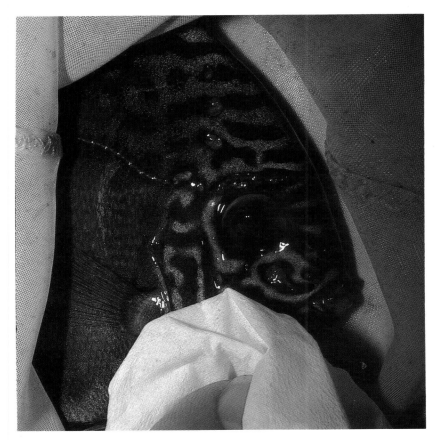

Discus and other large cichlids are subject to bacterial infections of the anterior lateral line. These can rapidly become uncontrollable if not treated immediately. The appropriate antibiotic is mixed into a heavy waterproof cream that is then spread over the infected areas. See your pet shop and veterinarian for details. Photos by the author.

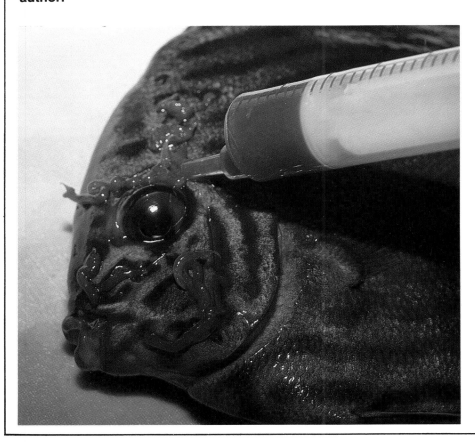

**MASOTEN**

A dose of 0.4 mg/L over two to three days is normal, but even higher doses can be tolerated by discus, though not by neons or barbs. Used for treatment of external trematodes and parasitic copepods, as well as leeches.

**NEGUVON**

Similar to Masoten, with a dose of 0.35 mg/L over two to three days.

**MALACHITE GREEN OXALATE**

Used for disinfection of eggs. Treat for one hour with 1-5 g/1000 L water. It can be used against many parasites and fungi.

**LEUKOMYCIN**

An injectable for abdominal dropsy in carp and for certain bacteria in a brief bath of two hours (160 mg/L). Such a bath should be repeated after six days.

**RESOCHIN**

This medicine for malaria is used to treat *Cryptocaryon*. A successful dose in discus is not certain. 40 mg/gallon (salt) water has been recommended.

**DRONCIT**

Medicine against tapeworms and leeches. Experience with salmon suggests a dose of 1-2 g/100 kg body weight.

**CLONT**

Used for a number of different protozoan parasites. The successful doses include 10,000 ppm fed over five days; 4 mg/L over three to four days; and 250 mg/20 gallons of water.

Above: Because the cream stays on in water, the antibiotic is allowed to work long enough to control the infection. Such discus may recover, but often they are permanently scarred. Photo by the author. Below: A syringe with a blunt cannula can be used to put worming drugs directly into the digestive system. Photos by the author.

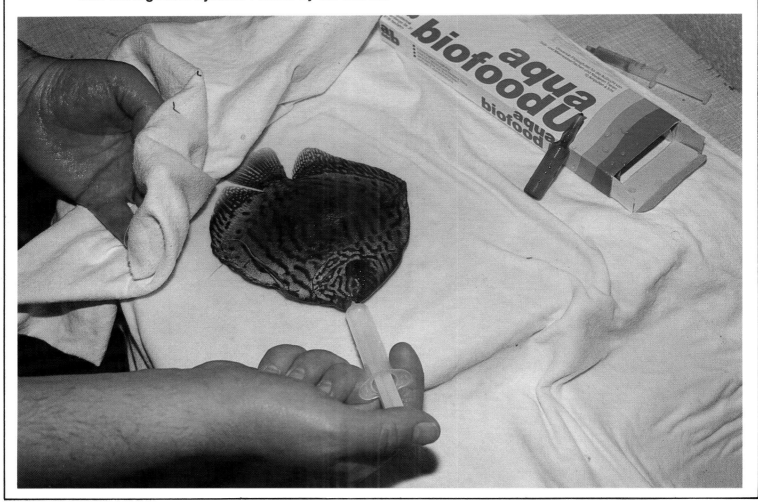

This discus has suffered considerable damage to the head and anterior lateral line due to a bacterial infection. If not treated the infection is likely to spread and may be terminal. Photo by the author.

## MANSONIL

A medicine against tapeworms used successfully with trout. Fed at 100 mg/kg body weight. The dose indicated in the literature is 10,000 ppm fed over three days.

## MEFAROL

A disinfectant for bacteria in the gills. Used especially in ponds with young trout. The dose is 20 ml Mefarol per 1000 L water for one hour. This treatment should be repeated two to three times a week.

## CONCURAT L

Used against intestinal worms at 300 mg/L. The medicine is fed to bloodworms that then are fed to the discus twice over three to five days.

Normally these medicines should not be left in the water more than two to three days. New activated carbon and a partial change of water are necessary after treatment.

### Specifics

Masoten may be given in high doses, even up to three times the normal dose. Short baths can be given up to ten times. The temperature of the water plays an important part in the treatment and should not be over 28°C (82°F). Any change in the temperature should be avoided, as at 33°C (91°F) and above the fish may die quickly. Other medicines also should not be used above 28°C (82°F).

Malachite green can lead to some problems as chemical reactions may occur after a few days of use. The solution should always be used fresh as it otherwise might destroy the slime of the fish. Any remnants in the water must be

Above: Because angelfish tend to be rather aggressive, they should not be housed with discus. Photo by the author.

Below: Although the caudal fin of this discus has been partially destroyed, it may regenerate if the water conditions are improved. Photo by the author.

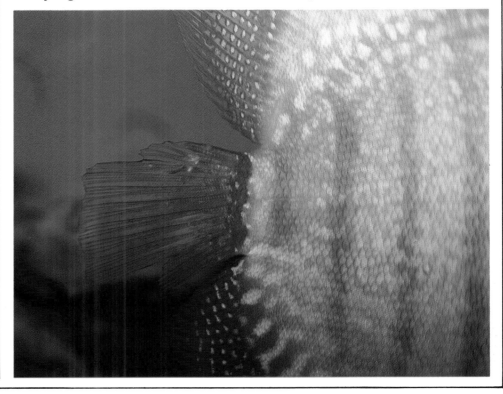

103

Above: These healthy young discus were killed by pH shock. Photo by the author. Below: New medications, such as waterproof cream, are constantly being made available to hobbyists. Check with your pet shop and veterinarian for medication details before attempting any "cures." Photo by the author.

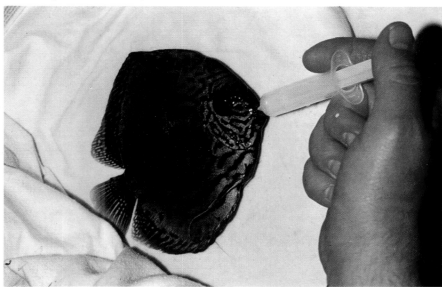

removed by filtering over activated carbon.

Resochin is a medicine not generally used for discus.

Droncit and Clont can be given orally through a plastic tube, but an overdose is possible. Treatment by injection is very ideal because of the very low weight of the fish. Another name for Clont is metronidazol, which comes in powder form. Your veterinarian will be able to give you these medicines if they are not available in your pet shop.

Mansonil and Mefarol ordinarily are not used on aquarium fishes.

Many of these medications would not be necessary if we would practice hygienic aquarium keeping, such as regular changes of water. Our tap water is full of pollutants

**Above:** The large black blotch at the base of the caudal fin of this Bangkok discus probably is a melanoma (cancer of the melanin or pigment-producing cells). In livebearers such melanomas commonly are fatal. Photo by the author.

**Below:** If the discus is too weak to eat when a condition such as worms is noticed, the medication may have to be injected by cannula. This requires practice and may be dangerous to the fish. Photo by the author.

Above: Pop-eye is more an indicator of poor conditions than an actual disease. Any of several causes, especially poor water, may lead to pop-eye. Below: Cannula injection also can be used to force-feed an ailing discus. Photos by the author.

that we cannot even detect, but in concentrations not harmful to man. However, we cannot be sure that even small concentrations are harmless to our fish. Such undetected pollutants may be one reason for deaths of discus.

**Salt**

Regular kitchen salt may not bring about miracles, but in small concentrations it may act as a preventative for some conditions and generally keep the fish healthier. It of course cannot be used if eggs or fry are in the aquarium.

At a concentration of 10-15 g/L in a bath for about 20 minutes, salt can be used to treat the gill flukes *Gyrodactylus* and *Dactylogyrus*.

Many retailers and importers use salt as a preventive measure, adding up to 500 g (17.5 ounces) of salt to 100 L (26 gallons) of water. The fish are kept in this solution one day, and on the second day one half of the water is changed.

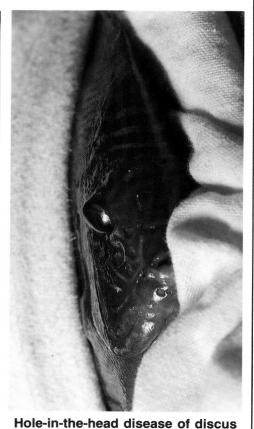

Hole-in-the-head disease of discus and other large cichlids is a mysterious disease that may have more than one cause. A small "pimple" on the head of the fish erupts and begins to grow into a deep crater that may penetrate the bone. If severe the condition can be fatal, but it also can be self-reversing and lead to nothing but minor scars. Although protozoans often have been cited as the cause, the disease responds to few medications and may be more a function of poor water quality with secondary viral, bacterial, and protozoan infections. Photo by the author.

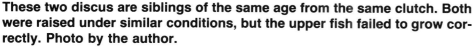

These two discus are siblings of the same age from the same clutch. Both were raised under similar conditions, but the upper fish failed to grow correctly. Photo by the author.

Left: A spectacular cobalt blue discus. Photo by the author.

The aquarium lighting causes the stripes of this brilliant blue male to shine bright red.

**This large male is the offspring of wild green discus. Photo by the author.**

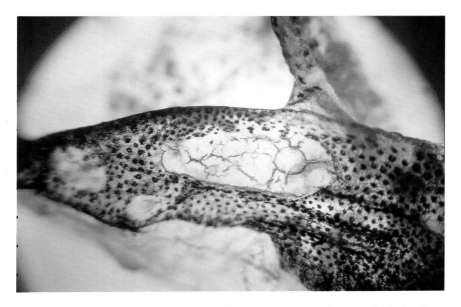

Above: A microscopic view of tissue damage due to hole-in-the-head disease. Treatment with antibiotics in waterproof cream (below) sometimes relieves the condition though it may not cure it. Photos by the author.

## A new mysterious sickness

Late in 1986 there appeared in Germany the first reports of mysterious deaths of discus. As they died after changes of water, it was supposed that pollutants in the water were the problem. These were thought to have come from an accident at a Swiss chemical factory that contaminated many central European water supplies.

The symptoms were as follows. The mucous membranes produced more and more mucus, the fish became blacker and blacker, they got shy, stayed in a corner of the aquarium, and became more and more apathetic. The production of mucus increased until it was sloughed off in large pieces. In extreme cases the fish died after 48 hours, but death during the next three days was more common. This was a progressive illness, but fish that survived slowly recovered. The rate of recovery depended on the cleanliness of the water and the number of fish being kept in the aquarium.

In addition to the discus, angelfishes, uarus, and tropheus appeared to be attacked, but not barbs, tetras, and salmon. In most cases the sickness clearly could not be due to parasites in the water.

Almost any chemical that decreases secondary infections (due to bacteria feeding on the decomposing mucus) will help to improve the condition of the fish. Sick fish with no other sickness, if put into absolutely clean aquaria, can be helped within hours. Their color will be clearer, but they still have thick mucus that can be seen on their sides for some days.

According to pet shop

reports, this sickness only occurs 24 to 48 hours after water changes made with tap water, indicating that this water contains substances dangerous to discus. Chemical analysis of the water has not detected any obvious cause, but perhaps the dangerous pollutant is present in such low quantities that it is difficult to detect. There also remains the possibility that a virus or bacterium is the cause, but so far tests have detected only bacteria typical of secondary infections.

The normal treatment is to put affected fish into fresh, clean water with no substrate. Filter the water through floss or foam and keep it at a temperature of 27 to 30°C (81-86°F). The drugs Neomycin

and Nitrofuran may help in supportive treatment as they dissolve the mucus and kill bacteria that would lead to secondary infections. Two grams of Neomycin sulfate are dissolved in 0.5 L (1 pint) of water and then added to 100 L (26 gallons).

The fish stay in the bath for three to five days and often recover after 36 hours. Additional feeding with vitamins is necessary. After being put back in their aquarium, the fish should continue to be treated for one or two weeks with Nitrofuran.

This treatment is totally ineffective if the fish have parasites such as intestinal worms or gill flukes, so that a preliminary microscopic examination for parasites is

**In discus, color often is in the eye of the beholder and also depends on the lighting. The lights used in this aquarium accentuate the red and blue colors of this sensational discus. Photo by the author.**

necessary. The presence of flagellates and other protozoans also prevents successful treatment. Protozoan parasites can be treated with 500 mg trypaflavin per 100 L (26 gallons) water and 5 mg malachite green in the water for three days. This mixture, however, is dangerous to the plants in the aquarium.

# Index

The author wishes to acknowledge the assistance of Messrs. Heymans and Musstopf. Heymans' photos appear on page 71, bottom and 108, bottom. Musstopf's photos appear on pages 27 top and 28 top. For further information about the drugs suggested in this book, the reader should consult the HANDBOOK OF FISH DISEASES by Dieter Untergasser, TS-123, published by TFH. It lists all of the modern treatments for aquarium fish diseases and advises the readers in England, Australia, New Zealand and the USA where to find the drugs recommended.